MY
MOTHER
WAS
RIGHT

MY MOTHER WAS RIGHT

HOW TODAY'S WOMEN RECONCILE WITH THEIR MOTHERS

Barbara McFarland • *Virginia Watson-Rouslin*

Jossey-Bass Publishers
San Francisco

The poem "Mothers and Daughters" by Pat Mora is reprinted with permission from the publisher of *Communion* (Houston: Arte Público Press–University of Houston, 1991).

Substantial discounts on bulk quantities of Jossey-Bass books are available to corporations, professional associations, and other organizations. For details and discount information, contact the special sales department at Jossey-Bass Inc., Publishers (415) 433-1740; Fax (800) 605-2665.

For sales outside the United States, please contact your local Simon & Schuster International Office.

Jossey-Bass Web address: http://www.josseybass.com

Library of Congress Cataloging-in-Publication Data

McFarland, Barabara.
    My mother was right: how today's women reconcile with their mothers/Barbara McFarland, Virginia Watson-Rouslin.
        p.   cm.
    Includes bibliographical references and index.
    ISBN 0-470-62335-7
    1. Mothers and daughters.   I. Watson-Rouslin, Virginia, date.
    II. Title.
HQ755.85.M365   1997
306.874'3—dc21   97-24510
                                                                         CIP

Contents

Preface

What a long, strange trip it has been, as Jerry Garcia, that balladeer of the 1960s through the 1990s, would say. Here we are, baby boomer women in our forties, and now, some of us have turned fifty, and we are changing our minds about our mothers. It is now occurring to us that the person we rebelled against, whom we used as a role model of how we would *not* like to lead our lives, and who upheld outmoded ideas on the place a woman should take in society and how she should behave, may not have been entirely wrong. She was not necessarily absolutely correct, mind you, but certainly we have now begun to seek a reconciliation with her on matters great and small. We see her nearing the end of her life (or perhaps she has already died, leaving us much more bereft than we ever thought we could be); we see ourselves entering middle age, some of us even seriously discussing facelifts and other efforts to disguise the work of Mother Nature. If we have had children of our own, their complaints about our standards and our being out of touch with reality have registered. We are beginning to see matters from our mother's point of view sometimes.

We women in midlife know the ground between our mothers and ourselves is shifting. We know we are admitting, even if at times somewhat reluctantly, to a vast storehouse of wisdom that entered our psyches through the words and actions of our mothers. Her oft-repeated homilies, those sound bites of motherly wisdom, which at one time would have caused us to roll our eyes and feel intense irritation, have taken on meaning.

"Your reputation is the most precious thing you own." This seemed so old-fashioned then, since it applied to our ability to be a "good girl" when it came to sex and boys, but now it has become a core value in our professional and personal lives.

"If it's worth doing, it's worth doing right." This favorite saying of hers usually popped out when what we were doing, whether it was folding the laundry or taking the garbage out, just did not measure up to her standards. Her criticism, intended or not, generated an intense conglomeration of emotions—anywhere from deep hurt to bitter rage. But now our lives are based on doing everything right, as reflected in the Superwoman syndrome.

"It's not what you say, it's how you say it." That's what Mom repeated ad nauseum. In talking to her, it seemed the only way to get through to her (or at least to get our own way with her), and now we use this advice quite successfully in our personal and professional negotiations.

"You'll thank me for this one day." Yes.

Little did we know that "one day" would rear its head so soon.

The Adventures of Midlife

Most people would agree that midlife is that point where we step out of the circle of our lives and reflect. Flickering images of faces and events from lifetimes ago surface. Generally these kinds of reflections surprise us and start slowly, somewhere around age forty or so, and then with each year, they take up more and more mental space and become more vivid.

Somewhere lurking among these images we notice a familiar face. Hard as we may try to brush her aside, she returns again and again. When we look in the mirror to comb our hair, somewhere a small voice whispers, "You have such pretty eyes! Why don't you cut those bangs so people can see them?" (advice our hairdresser agrees with). Or, on opening the brown glass bottle of McCormick's vanilla, we are greeted by an aroma that floods us with a picture of her standing in the kitchen at the chipped Formica counter, with the KitchenAid whirring. She hands the little girl beside her a spatula full of white, sticky dough to lick.

Not all of the blinking of our eyes or the shaking of our heads will deny our mother's rightful place in this midlife process of reflection. We simply can't ponder our own lives without her being there.

No one would deny that mothers and daughters are the most talked-about, written-about, and maligned of all human relationships. One psychologist refers to the mother-daughter relationship as the world's greatest love affair.

Betty Friedan's 1963 book, *The Feminine Mystique*, started baby boomer women on the road to "independence," raised fundamental questions about the kinds of lives our mothers had led (and the narrow paths we saw as our only routes to independence), and gave voice to the inner dissatisfaction of women. But its aftermath took us to the other side, where our brothers had been directed: a side that fostered patriarchal values, such as the need to achieve, to succeed, to compete, to be independent.

At midlife, many of us have begun to realize that in some ways, we are right back where we started. Inner dissatisfaction rears its head again, only this time we are fearful of what it might be trying to tell us. We look at our lives and wonder why we aren't feeling any better than the women Friedan wrote about in the 1960s. This is especially frightening since we believed that competing, succeeding, and living lives unlike our mother's would fulfill us. Maybe what we were looking for was closer at hand, after we had taken our long journeys; our mothers' advice and wisdom was there for the taking.

As our mothers approach death and we our own aging, we daughters are beginning to see our mothers and ourselves from a different perspective.

Working women at midlife are shifting to a new consciousness, able to embrace and truly value our feminine nature yet maintain a reasonable appreciation of the other side—the side that values the qualities of rationality, competition, independence, and achievement. We are discovering that we do not need to devalue one set of values in order to hold on to the other. As we grow in wisdom, we are beginning to realize that careers need to grow out of *who* we are and not the other way around. This new consciousness is transforming us so that we can make choices for our lives that truly come from within our very nature, our center.

Midlife is that bittersweet process during which we look for the truth within ourselves. And for women, a critical step in this process begins with understanding and reconfiguring our relationship with our mothers. This must encompass not only appreciating and accepting our mothers as women and as "good-enough" mothers but also forgiving them. Most of the time they did their best, as we are trying to do with our own daughters. This process also means that we acknowledge the feminine nature we share with our mothers. By doing so, we come home—home to that place within ourselves where we experience peace and finally achieve self-acceptance. In coming to terms with this primary relationship, we are able to come to terms with ourselves and then move into the next phase of our life's journey. Some of us may take our moms along; others may need to leave her behind. Regardless of the choice, we travel more easily and freely and with much less baggage.

An Awakening

As two boomer daughters ourselves, this book emerged from our relationship with our own mothers. We both came of age with two vigorously competing visions of womanhood: that of our mothers and that of feminism, that of Ladies' Home Journal and Ms. magazine, and Helen Gurley Brown versus Gloria Steinem. The journeys we have taken in our relationships with our moms have been dominated by numerous detours into uncharted territories, all in a direction heading away from them and what their lives represented. Then one day, when we were in the middle of our lives, we discovered that we could no longer keep wandering.

The subjects of our long conversations changed when midlife hit us. We found ourselves reflecting more, sharing the twists and turns of our lives and how we both got to be in Cincinnati, doing what we were doing—one a psychologist, the other, at the time, a public affairs officer for the Canadian government. In the midst of our reveries about our careers, siblings, husbands, and son, no matter how much we tried to minimize it, we could not escape the dominant role our moms had played in our lives. We were struck by the strength, stamina, and courage of these two women, Anne and Marjorie, and of the values they fought hard to instill in us.

As we talked about our mothers, we were also struck by the similarities in the tone and temperament of our relationship with them in spite of the very different lives our mothers led. One was a homemaker with a ninth-grade education; the other was an elementary school teacher who, although also a homemaker, returned to teaching when the youngest of her children was in junior high. It didn't seem to make much difference what our mothers did. We just knew that we wanted to have different kinds of lives than they did. We wanted to participate fully in the "real" world, where we would be valued and recognized.

Naturally we gave no credence to the social context in which they lived their lives or the expectations everyone had of them—including their children—some of which were quite unreasonable. We grew up in Chicago and Calgary, Alberta, Canada, in middle-class homes that were very much a part of a culture that valued productivity, competitiveness, the almighty dollar, and the jobs our fathers held, but that devalued homemaking activities. This background, along with our perception (as well as the reality) that our moms had less power overall in their relationships, influenced our rejection of our mother's lifestyles—a rejection that in large part was based on our culture's dominant patriarchal value system.

For much of the time as we were growing up, we consciously looked for something different to make of our lives. In Barbara's case, it was an "equal and opposite reaction" to the very traditional life her mother had led. She was quite clear in her mind about that.

In Virginia's case, it was not as well defined, but she did know that she had to leave her home and move to a city over two thousand miles from where she had grown up to find some answers.

We thus traveled away from our mothers, literally and figuratively, hoping to find another way to be full-fledged women. We both embraced the women's movement, as it was called, and took a look at all the questions Gloria Steinem, Betty Friedan, and Kate Millett were raising. At the same time, we tried to live a reasonably normal life, marrying, having children (for Barbara), and pursuing careers. All the while, we kept looking back at our mothers and their lives, as a way to make sure our paths were nowhere near theirs.

When we began to talk about this book, we realized that we'd begun to change our minds about our mothers. In Barbara's case, she saw that her mom's focus on child rearing and domestic production had been a significant achievement, even though this contribution could not be measured in a progression of career moves, promotions, or dollars and cents. In Virginia's case, it was more complex, since her mother, while clearly focused on raising her children, had also enjoyed a career as a teacher and an association with a wide variety of friends outside of her traditional family. Her strength in all these areas had meant that she did have a credibility beyond the traditional structure; but, for Virginia, the path had to be wider still. Nonetheless, both of us found that at midlife, we began to appreciate the feminine values both our mothers' lives represented, and we began to feel more centered. Our many conversations and shared insights gave birth to this book.

The Study

Our approach was less of a formal study than a method by which women going through midlife could tell their stories about their relationships with their mothers. Since mothers have historically been blamed for all that ails us, we wanted to focus on the more positive aspects of this relationship, especially since we believe that baby boomer women who, much like us, had once discounted their mothers were now beginning to appreciate what their mothers had to offer. We wanted to listen to women now in midlife describe their mother and their new, changing relationship with her. We were the tape recorder, and sometimes the interpreter.

With one of us a practicing psychologist, not only were the survey responses interpreted to some degree from this perspective, but general relational dynamics were also discussed in the light of this clinical experience. The other author, a former journalist and journalism instructor, came to the project with a more social-political background and tended to interpret data in a broader social context. We think that this diversity has kept the book balanced.

Although this is not an academic book, we have made an effort to survey the literature and document some historical and statistical facts relating to the times in which both we and our mothers have lived. But what was always paramount to the project was the telling of stories. One hundred seventy women shared with us the details of their mothers' lives: how they got along with them then and get along now, and how they view this relationship.

In seeking respondents, we not only wanted average working women like ourselves but also women whose accomplishments have gone beyond the ordinary. Of the 170 respondents, 10 of them fall into this latter category.

The highly accomplished women were selected as the result of a seven-month-long search. We started with women we knew and then networked with other friends and associates. Given that one of us is a Canadian, we wanted to include women from this country in addition to American women. We were delighted that Canadian women of great achievement were intrigued by the project and were so willing to talk about their mothers, even though the moms of two of our interviewees, Maureen Kempston Darkes and Karen Kain, had recently died.

We contacted well over seventy publicists, agents, and executive assistants, by telephone, fax, and the good old-fashioned letter, who worked for these women, because we knew they would have

something special to add. They labored under the same circumstances we did, yet still managed to achieve a great deal in their professional lives. We wanted to know about their moms. We ranged
far afield, from golfer Betsy King to Mae Jamison, the first U.S. black
female astronaut. Some turned us down through their agents, but
others called and spoke with us themselves. One, the producer of a
hit television series, called to say how interesting she thought the
project was, but she had a troubled and painful relationship with
her mother and thus did not feel as if she fit the general profile and
did not want to talk about her mother for publication. She made a
point of saying she would not do anything to hurt her mother. That
was a theme heard in many of our interviews: the desire to protect
our mothers. Another television producer and former anchorwoman
said through an assistant that she was thinking about writing a book
on the same topic. The women who agreed to be interviewed form
an incredibly diverse and accomplished group.

When we could, we interviewed these women in person, and
when not, by telephone. These interviews lasted from one and a
half to two hours and basically covered the questions from our survey (reprinted in Appendix A), augmented by these women's special achievements and how their mothers influenced the paths they
took in life. Locations ranged from quiet offices, to piano studios,
to a very noisy Spanish restaurant, where our tape recorder sat
beneath a blaring speaker of Spanish music and lusty maracas, making the transcription a challenge.

As for the 160 other respondents, we found them by advertising in local newspapers in Chicago, San Francisco, Denver,
Cincinnati, and the *New York Review of Books*. We posted flyers in
bookstores and coffee shops and enlisted our relatives and friends
from around the United States and Canada to do the same. As a
result, we received over 300 calls, with 160 women completing our
survey.

We would have preferred to have spoken with each respondent
in person, but because of time constraints, we could not. Instead,

we conducted follow-up interviews by telephone on fifteen of the surveys and met with five respondents in a group format. We selected these five women based on their responses to some of the questions we posed that we wanted to explore in more depth. As it turned out, they were a well-rounded group: a physician, a director of a social service agency, a full-time mother of four, a Ph.D. candidate in history, and an artist-photographer.

When we began talking to the respondents, whether by telephone or in person, individually or in our group, we were struck by the fact that daughters are no strangers to one another. All one has to do is mention the "M" word, and the usual facade of social propriety in initial meetings drops quickly to a relaxed, intimate conversation usually reserved for best friends. This was the tone of each of our interviews. When women talk about their mothers, something mystical happens.

During all of our interviews, our conversations were filled with laughter, tears, painful silences, thoughtful smiles, and an overall tuning into the emotions of one another. In talking about our mothers, nothing less can be expected. Although we had never met any of these women before, we became intimately connected through our mothers for a brief period of time.

Who are the women whose stories make up this book? Sixty-seven percent come primarily from the Midwest, 21 percent from the West, 4 percent from the East, 3 percent from the South, and 5 percent from Canada. Eighty-nine percent are Caucasian, 7 percent are African American, 2 percent call themselves Native American, and 2 percent are Hispanic. Their ages range from thirty-five to fifty-two, the average age being forty-three years of age. Sixty percent of the women are married, 14 percent are single, 22 percent are divorced, and 4 percent are widowed.

Thirty-four percent have no children, 61 percent have 1 to 3 children, and 5 percent have 4 or 5. No one reported having more than 6 kids, although this was not true for their mothers. Daughters averaged 2 children, while their mothers averaged 3.6.

We have an array of religious beliefs, encompassing "recovering Catholic," Orthodox Greek, Jewish, New Thought, Buddhist, Hindu, transcendentalist, and others, with the largest denomination listing themselves as Roman Catholics.

Women who responded to the survey were highly educated; no respondent had less than a high school education. In fact, 28 percent attended college, though they did not receive a degree; 33 percent have college degrees; and a full 28 percent have graduate degrees. Eleven percent have a high school diploma.

Although our respondents' mothers also had relatively high levels of education (compared with the general population during the 1940s and 1950s), their daughters have outscored them considerably on this criterion, but very much because their mothers urged them to do so. Fourteen percent of our daughters' mothers did not graduate from high school, but 47 percent do have their high school diplomas. Fifteen percent of the mothers have a college degree, and 17 percent have some college. Seven percent went on to obtain graduate degrees, and one mother was awarded her graduate degree in social work at age sixty.

The vast majority of the daughters in our survey are working, most in professional occupations. Thirty percent of their mothers worked in full-time nonprofessional jobs, 19 percent were full-time homemakers, and the remainder moved in and out of the labor force as circumstances at home dictated. Their careers, however, were dictated less by choice than by necessity.

As for where our respondents and their mothers lived and their degree of contact, 29 percent of our respondents lived in the same city as their moms, 31 percent lived in the same state but different towns, and 40 percent lived in different states or provinces. In spite of all the angst and sometimes difficulties (in the past and in the present), respondents and their mothers kept in quite close touch. Twenty-five percent talk to their moms every day by telephone, 49 percent talk to her once or twice a week by telephone, with the remaining respondents having more irregular telephone contact. Thirty-one percent of the respondents initiate the telephone calls,

14 percent of their mothers do, and 55 percent report that these are equally initiated.

Seven percent of the respondents see their moms four to seven times a week, 22 percent see them one to three times a week, 19 percent see them a few times a month, and 52 percent see them one to eight times a year (a healthy average, considering the majority do not live in the same city or town).

To protect confidentiality, we have changed respondents' names, but everything else about each respondent is as she told it to us. There are absolutely no composites, or people we have created from several respondents' input.

We are deeply grateful for the openness that our respondents and interviewees demonstrated in sharing about their mothers' stories and their relationships with their mothers. Those who responded to our toll-free number and filled out the survey probably spent up to two hours answering fifty-two questions, the majority of which were essay type. We appreciate the time they spent, and we hope they appreciate the result.

Overview of the Book

The book's eleven chapters have been divided into three parts. Part One lays the groundwork and places the daughters and mothers in social and historical context. In Chapter One, we discuss motherhood as it is idealized and the particular challenges mothers and daughters face in shaping a relationship within a masculine-driven culture. We present a framework that delineates three types of mother-daughter relationships: the Untraveled Daughter, the Wandering Daughter, and the Prodigal Daughter. In Chapter Two we look back to the 1940s, 1950s, 1960s, and 1970s and present a snapshot view of both the times in which our moms raised us, as well as the times in which we came of age.

Parts Two and Three present the results of our interviews and surveys. Our chapter titles reflect the clichés most often heard by boomer daughters from their mothers. Our mothers had an amazing array of homilies and bon mots that they scattered across our lives, many were intended to teach us something, and in as few words as possible. Many of these came from *their* mothers. We wonder (but do not know) how many of us are handing these off to our daughters. In Appendix B you can enjoy this collection of advice, which is easily subdivided into themes ranging from men to manners.

Part Two specifically focuses on the gifts our mothers gave us— those things she was right about or had a special wisdom about, which were most valued by our respondents and interviewees. Chapter Three focuses on the importance of getting an education, or "something to fall back on," as many of our mothers saw it. That critical direction laid an important foundation for nearly every woman whose story we tell. They may have hated their mothers for nagging or rejected her advice to study more traditional subjects at college, but now they are grateful. In Chapter Four we look at the issue of independence, or "standing on your two feet." Mother taught us this, though she often lived to regret it. We took this foundation and made our lives less dependent on men than hers had been. (Some of our respondents think they need to move back to the center on this, however.) Chapter Five explores the lessons our mothers taught us about being mothers. Chapter Six presents our moms' influence on our spirituality and creativity, and Chapter Seven deals with how they civilized us, teaching the importance of manners and thoughtfulness not only with friends and family but with the community at large.

Part Three brings the relationship to where it is today and discusses the issues most often expressed by our respondents and interviewees. Chapter Eight focuses on the power of the gene pool. Respondents share their earliest awarenesses of the oft-dreaded mother likenesses and similarities—whether these idiosyncrasies are as simple as how we keep house or as disturbing as seeing our own hand morphing into our mother's. Chapter Nine presents the controversial topic of mothers as friends and describes some tools and strategies for redefining our relationships with our moms. Chapter

Ten addresses the role reversal that daughters are now feeling as they nurture and care for their aging mothers, as well as how our respondents feel about life without their moms. Chapter Eleven deals with the issue of reconciliation. Respondents share how they have been able to achieve a sense of peace with their moms. The epilogue looks to the next generation, to see what our daughters think about us.

We realize that the mother-daughter relationship is complex and intricately unique to each pair. In spite of its uniqueness, we hope that this book, through the voices of the women who contributed, gives all our readers some inspiration and guidance that lead to a greater appreciation of themselves and their mothers.

Cincinnati, Ohio   Barbara McFarland
July 1997   Virginia Watson-Rouslin

To the Dressel sisters, Annie, Stefka, and Sabina
(BMc)

To my mother, Marjorie Watson Prieur
(VWR)

Acknowledgments

When we began this book, we had only a vague idea of how much work would be involved, much less how many people whose paths we would cross would offer us help in completing this project. Of course, our first acknowledgments are to our mothers, Annie and Marjorie, both of whom looked with some trepidation on the subject matter, but who nonetheless gave us their wholehearted support in our quest to survey women and pull it together in a book. All Marjorie said was, "Well, be gentle."

There are other people who played a critical role in helping us make this book come to pass:

The high-achieving women we chose to interview spoke honestly about their mothers in spite of the deeply personal nature of the subject and the fact that two—Maureen Kempston Darkes of General Motors and ballerina Karen Kain—had just lost their mothers. The respondents all were remarkably candid and helped us fill out the vast canvas that was our subject matter. Katherine Hancock Ragsdale, who never met us in person, nevertheless gladly spoke for several hours long distance about her own mom. One hundred sixty other women finished the long survey and then took a leap of faith in us and returned their surveys to us; this book could not have been written without them. Most of these women also gave us their telephone numbers in case we wanted to follow up with a call; to those with whom we spoke, thank you. We also thank the other 150 or so women who called and asked for the surveys but did not return them. It did indicate to us the high level of interest in the subject. Then there were the wonderful women we found in Cincinnati, who had completed the surveys and represented all the ranges of feelings about their mothers that we wanted to tap. They eagerly agreed to set aside a good portion of a warm Saturday in August in order to meet with us in a group session. They were good-natured about passing around the small tape recorder and repeating their name every time they spoke, to help us in transcribing the tapes. They were honest, funny, and insightful. When we last saw them, they were huddled outside after the session, engaged in intense conversation. They'd never met one another before. To the young women who set aside their Saturday morning in February to talk about their baby boomer mothers, thanks for reminding us that our generation too has work to do with our daughters.

Were it not for Kris Nichols, who deciphered three hundred names and addresses from our voice mail and then set about sending out these surveys, we might still be running ads and sorting through surveys. That was only part of what Kris did, and we thank her for her support, patience, and ability to keep us calmly anchored during our more frenzied moments. She was important in helping us with our computer deficits, which are legion. To Mary Herbst, we give thanks for her unwavering support and her strong interest in the project. She did a beautiful job transcribing over fifty hours of audiotapes and revisions and then helped with the preparation of the final manuscript. To Peggy Sheets, we are grateful for her cheerful willingness to do research and library work, as well as data tabulation.

To the friends, colleagues, and family members who supported us and willingly put up flyers and distributed our surveys but especially to our dearest, long-time friends—Michelle Cook in Red Deer, Alberta; Betts Chamberlain Top in Canon Falls, Minnesota; and Alice Tondryk Benedict in Chicago—we are truly thankful. Thanks also to Cameron Lawrence in Louisville; George Costaris,

Dennis Moore, and Mary Lynn Becker at the Canadian Consulate General in Detroit; Henry Wells at the Canadian Consulate General in Dallas; Anne Garneau from the Canadian Consulate General in New York; and Gerry Foley at the Canadian Consulate General in Minneapolis, who was instrumental in persuading writer Carol Shields to set aside time in her busy schedule for an interview with two unknown writers. Thanks also to Larry Cox of Kentucky Senator Mitch McConnell's office.

I (BMc) extend deep appreciation to my sister, Marilyn Krutz, for recruiting women in Atlanta to fill out surveys; to my son, Casey Ryan, for his continued encouragement and support; to my spouse, Harold, who has let me pursue my dreams; and to the other Caseys of my life—my dad and my brother—just because.

I (VWR) thank my husband, Bill, for his help and support, for finding the right software, for ferrying disks back and forth to Barbara, and for his belief that the book would get done and be a great success. I hope he's right! Finally, to Dad: although he has been gone since 1979, he was a writer, and I would have loved to be able to show him my first book. It took awhile, Dad, but better late than never.

Finally, our thanks to Jossey-Bass Publishers, to Alan Rinzler for believing in the topic and to Barbara Hill, who helped us so much in organizing our ideas and with the final structure of the book. Her enthusiasm for the project meant that she was responsive and thoughtful; she did a wonderful job of separating the wheat from the chaff. Her job was followed up by Bev Miller, an exceptional copyeditor who polished and tidied and asked us questions about phrases and arguments we'd begun to accept as gospel—until she made us rethink the matter. And thank you to everyone else on the staff at Jossey-Bass, including Margaret Sebold, Margaret Chou, and Kim Corbin, whose marketing and publicity skills will help ensure that as many women as possible hear of our work.

B. Mc.

V. W.-R.

MOTHERS and DAUGHTERS

The arm-in-arm-mother-daughter stroll
in villages and shopping malls
evenings and weekends
the w a l k - t a l k slow,
arm-in-arm
    around the world.

Sometimes they feed one another
memories sweet as hot bread
and lemon tea. Sometimes it's mother-stories
The young one can't remember:

"When you were new, I'd nest you
in one arm, while I cooked,
whisper, what am I to do with you?"

Sometimes it's tug-
-of-war that started in the womb
the fight for space
the sharp jab deep inside
as the weight shifts,
arm-in-arm
    around the world
always the bodytalk,
always the recipes
hints for feeding
more with less.

Pat Mora
Communion, Arte Público Press, Houston, 1991, p. 79

MY
MOTHER
WAS
RIGHT

Part I

In the Beginning

The Journey

I rebelled against my mother starting about the age of eighteen, I think. I lived a very alternative life, and I just rejected everything that came from her. And it took me a good ten or fifteen years to come back to some of her values.

Gwen, forty-seven-year-old
photographer from Cincinnati

We were the first generation to grow up under the influence of more than one mother (not counting extended family). We had our very own flesh-and-blood moms as well as the ones who, with a turn of a knob, visited our living rooms weekly: June Cleaver, Betty Anderson, and Harriet Nelson. And when we compared our real mothers to our television moms, we were often terribly disappointed. Where was that freshly starched apron? And what about those pearls, which framed a lovely, serene face glowing with just the right amount of pancake makeup? How come our television moms spoke to their kids with melodious tones of sweetness and light—their conversations devoid of nags and threats, arguments and cold silences? How come our moms didn't seem as joyful, even-tempered, patient, and kind? And why weren't we as happy and well adjusted as our television siblings: Beaver and Wally; Betty, "Kitten," and Bud; Rick and Dave? They were pimple free, had lots of friends and dates, and knew just what to say at the right time. It was *her* fault . . . all her fault. As we munched our Cheetos, licking the salt and crumbs from our yellow-stained fingers, we often fantasized how our lives could be different if only our moms were more like the ones we stared at in those magical boxes.

Motherhood Idealized

We were the first generation to witness the mythology of motherhood played out before our very eyes. Since the beginning of time, mothers have always been held to incredibly high expectations, responsible for everything from our self-esteem to our attitudes about sex. If mother cares too much, she is overprotective or, in the jargon of the 1990s, "codependent"; if she does not care enough, she is cold and withholding. A mother is rarely, if ever, good enough.

Although psychoanalytic theory has done much to advance our understanding of human behavior, it has also done much to cultivate a mythology about motherhood that, depending on how a mother interacts with her developing child, either keeps her high on a pedestal or plummets her to the depths of hell. And we all know what end of the spectrum Harriet, June, and Betty fell into: perfection personified.

Nancy Friday's best-selling book of 1977, *My Mother/My Self*, takes us to the other end of the spectrum: how our mothers failed us. Her book is generously peppered with the philosophy and quotations from experts within the psychoanalytic camp, all of whom eloquently speak of the ideal mother, the theoretically created mother who should be able to breast-feed and potty train us perfectly. These experts talk about our mothers' inadequacies, unmet dependency needs, and projections, and of our corresponding anger and resentments. The psychobabble of symbiosis, guilt, narcissistic gratification, and separation and individuation suffuses the book.

Whenever motherhood is worshipped or vilified, the different challenges in mothering male and female children are rarely noted, except maybe in the more recent clinical journals. In our culture, successful mothering is most often judged by how "independent" the offspring are of their mothers (parents) as they move into adulthood. This criterion, however, becomes somewhat fuzzy when it comes to girls.

The Art of Mothering a Female

In our culture, a healthy adult is thought to be a person fully emancipated from parents, especially one who has cut the apron strings, both emotionally and economically. Psychologists refer to this stage of development as "separation" or "individuation." Anyone who fails to follow this ideal developmental path and lingers with his or her mother past childhood is at odds with social expectations. In fact, in psychological jargon, such a person is generally considered to be exhibiting regressive tendencies and is typically described as dependent, weak, and passive. Freud and his colleagues would have us believe that distancing from our mothers is a critical stage in our development into healthy adulthood.

Clearly mothers of daughters, as well as the daughters themselves, have a particular challenge in successfully achieving this task, especially since it goes against the very grain of women's natural developmental style, which is relational in makeup. Typically the mother-daughter relationship is permeated by feelings of guilt and shame, anger and resentment, in large part because both women are struggling to relate to each other in a culture that favors independence, competitiveness, separation-individuation, achievement, and a one-up relational style. But women are basically empathic, and their makeup favors mutuality, cooperation, affiliation, and connection. That means that mothers and daughters cannot break the bond that exists between them any more than an orchestra could play without a conductor. The field of psychology has come to a fuller appreciation and understanding of the challenges that mothers and daughters in our culture face through the research being conducted by such notable clinicians as Jean Baker Miller at the Stone Center at Wellesley College.

Women Are Different

Miller wrote her groundbreaking *Toward a New Psychology of Women* in 1976. In it, she recognizes a different starting point for women's development: "One central feature is that women stay with, build on and develop in a context of connections with others. Indeed, women's sense of self becomes very much organized around being able to make and then to maintain affiliations and relationships. Eventually, for many women the threat of disruption of connections is perceived not as just a loss of a relationship but as something closer to a total loss of self." Baker Miller goes on to emphasize that women honor affiliations more highly than they do self-enhancement.

Harvard University professor Carol Gilligan supports this thesis in her book, *In a Different Voice:*

> Relationships, and particularly issues of dependency, are experienced differently by women and men. For boys and men, separation and individuation are critically tied to gender identity since separation from the mother is essential for the development of masculinity. For girls and women, issues of femininity or feminine identity do not depend on the achievement of separation from the mother or on the progress of individuation. Since masculinity is defined through separation while femininity is defined through attachment, male gender identity is threatened by intimacy while female gender identity is threatened by separation.

Conflicts in the mother-daughter relationship are intensified given this female relational style, although this is changing given the new perspective on women's development. In order to both individuate and pursue self-enhancement as dictated by cultural standards and values, many of us rejected our mothers and those qualities of womanhood that their lives most often reflected.

We are beginning to realize that we cannot and need not break the bond with our mothers. We are awakening to the possibility of transforming our relationship with her and at the same time integrating those qualities we (and the wider culture) once saw as so limiting.

Although the attachment to her is enduring, it is also forever changing, which is what makes the relationship so complex and fascinating. There is a continual negotiation and renegotiation of space between us and our mothers—not too much distance, so that it does not feel as if we are abandoning each other, and not too much closeness, so that it does not feel as if we are suffocating each other. By understanding and appreciating the relational nature of women, we will be better able to appreciate fully our mothers and ourselves, as well as that mysterious space that flows between us.

The Road Most Traveled

Since the moment she pushed us out of her body, we daughters have been on a journey in our relationship with our mother. For some of us, it has been short and sweet, for others long and arduous, and for others tumultuous and even dangerous. It is during midlife that the journey has led most of us back to her—to an appreciation of her not only as a mother, but mostly as a woman and a person. We have come home to a space between our mother and ourself where we are beginning to feel comfortable. We realize that our need to be connected with her, as well as with others, is a quality within ourselves to be treasured and cherished, although it is sometimes devalued by the culture.

Of course, this relationship does not end here; as with most other things in life, it is just another beginning. The mother-daughter relationship continues to take shape, stretching and growing until the remaining person of the pair takes her last breath, and even then, it continues to live through our daughters. It is a work of art in progress, as long as we do not continue to see her through the eyes of our younger selves or judge her through the cultural lens of the perfect mother.

In America, motherhood is sacred. But the reality is there are mothers who are neglectful and abusive, and do not deserve the privilege of having children. The children of such mothers have greater challenges to deal with as they move through life. Although this book is intended to focus on our reconciliation with our mothers, we thought it important to include the surveys we received from women still traveling the road and often in a great deal of pain. Not all women come home, nor should they. For some, it is better to keep right on traveling.

We believe that as women read this book, and think and talk about their mothers from the perspective of what they did right, they will be struck, as we were, by the courage, the wisdom, and the tenacity of the women who bore us. This is not an unrealistic idealization and a 1990s version of Betty, June, and Harriet, because, along with this respect and admiration, we are very much aware of our mothers' shortcomings. We have come to love them, warts and all.

The Travelers on the Road

Through both our interviews and survey results, we discovered that although each respondent has been on a unique journey in her relationship with her mother, as a group they generally tended to fall into three types, which we call the Wandering Daughter, the Prodigal Daughter, and the Untraveled Daughter. (These are simply used as descriptors and not as any clinical type.)

Wandering Daughters are still traveling, not ready or willing to come home because their anger and resentments over early childhood wounds will not let them. They carry their anger like a banner, waving it righteously, or hold it deep within the recesses of their hearts. In either case, they cling to these negative and painful emotions often to justify why they can never go home, why they can never see their mothers in any positive light. And although the psychologists of the world would judge such behavior as a sign of neurosis, we prefer to view it as a part of the trip.

Although the pain that women who were neglected or abused by their mothers cannot be discounted, it might be simpler to acknowledge that these mothers may have lacked the nurturing *skills* necessary to care for their daughters. This deficit deserves the anger, not so much the mothers.

The *Prodigal Daughters* are daughters who, like us, discounted their mothers, their words, how they lived their lives, and vowed to be nothing like them. These are the women who experienced anger, guilt, and motherly disapproval. The road has smoothed out, and they are beginning to see their mothers differently. This is not to say that they do not still experience these feelings. It is just that now these emotions are tempered with humor, perspective, and self-confidence. In discussing the road back, Prodigal Daughters talk about one key factor that allowed them to turn home: forgiveness. They were able to forgive their mothers and themselves for being less than perfect.

There is a softening, a mellowing, a rediscovery of their mothers as women who did contribute something wonderful to the texture of their daughters' lives. These daughters are now beginning not only to appreciate the traditional, so-called "relational" qualities of caretaking, nurturance, and cooperation but also to deeply respect these qualities as an important part of the human experience.

Untraveled Daughters generally have had a positive relationship with their mothers from the very beginning of the trip. They always thought their mothers were right and have, for the most part, been able to appreciate them. These daughters either did not have to take the journey or, if they did, it was a short and sweet one. Unlike psychologists and psychiatrists who would characterize these women as "idealizing" their mothers, we have found it to be much less complicated than that. They simply got along with their moms. It is hard to pinpoint exactly what contributes to this type of relationship. We tend to think it may be as simple as that of compatible temperaments or personality styles.

What does it matter when one woman can simply say that she gets along with another woman, can actually love her and not be in some major conflict with her? Our culture has a hard time with women, especially mothers and daughters, whose relationships are characterized by harmony and appreciation.

The Wandering Daughter

The Wandering Daughter is someone who experiences a mix of painful emotions toward her mother for her failures as a mother and/or for not having gained her mother's approval. As a forty-eight-year-old college graduate and mother of two says, "Our relationship has never been all that great. I'll be seventy years old and still not pleasing her." There is no real joy or companionship in these relationships. The dominant emotional markers within the Wandering Daughter relationship are outrage, anger, excessive guilt, hurt, disappointment, and sadness.

Suzi, a thirty-nine-year-old married and "unhappy Catholic" from Chicago, is the middle of three children and is a secretary. Her parents are still alive and have been married for forty-three years. Her mother, age sixty-four and retired, worked during her entire married life as a "clerk for various trucking companies as a union employee." Suzi reports that she and her mother are now having more problems than ever: "She's bitter, cynical, and hateful toward everything and everyone. She's just unhappy with life." Still, Suzi drops in on her mother once a week to "talk if she will," and she initiates most of the telephone contacts between them. "She's made all of her children depend on her financially. She's always given what money can buy—on her conditions. But when we don't jump through her hoops, she cuts us off."

In responding to our question, "What is the greatest piece of advice your mother gave you?" Suzi replies, "My mother doesn't give advice; she doesn't want to interfere. She just asks, 'Why did you do that? See where it got you.'" At the end of the survey, Suzi says of her mother, "The worst thing she gave me was life. This is hell. I am so happy I don't have a daughter to continue this pattern."

Interestingly enough, in response to how she has been most influenced by her mother, Suzi identifies the area of relationships. Her mom told her, "You don't need a man if you have your own career." Other respondents viewed this advice, although not necessarily said in the same fashion, as a positive contribution in their lives, since it encouraged their independence and ongoing education. Like a cracked mirror, intense anger can prevent us from seeing our mothers without distortion. There are aspects of her that, depending on the view we take, can be very useful in our lives.

Suzi seems to be just as unhappy as she thinks her mother is. Her anger and resentment will continue to fester until she is able to forgive her mother for her shortcomings and focus on the more positive times (no matter how few) they have together or decide to limit her contact with her mom altogether.

Issues of Neglect and Abuse

Many Wandering Daughters have been verbally or physically abused (or both) at the hands of their moms or their dads or stepdads, to the blind eye of their mothers. Blanche, a thirty-eight-year-old married mother of two teenagers, says, "When I was a teenager, my mother yelled. I sat and said nothing. I cried silently to myself. She still screams or talks very negatively, and I don't say anything. I keep away. I've learned to stay away from her and not discuss much with her. Maybe I've built a shield to protect myself."

A thirty-five-year-old divorced mother who works full-time assesses her relationship with her mother in this way: "When I was a teenager I only hated my mother part of the time. Now I hate her all of the time. She puts me down. Calls me a slut and a whore. Not one item of clothing I buy for my daughter is right. Nothing I do is good or right. She always tells me what to do."

And then there is Beth, who describes the abuse she received from her mother as more covert. She hand-wrote us a fourteen-page letter presenting a sad view of a tormented relationship with her mother. Beth is forty-seven years old and married, with two adult sons. Her mother, at seventy-nine, was one of seven children born to Polish immigrants who settled in the Midwest. Beth says, "I idolized my mother throughout my teens and twenties. She was literally a god to me. I saw her as hard working, strong, attractive, bright, and articulate."

It was only in her thirties that Beth became increasingly aware of the dysfunction in her family: "The great coincidence of my life, a family counseling center opened across the street from my home. I began working there, learning, deciphering, and integrating every piece of information that came to me." As the office manager, Beth was able to benefit from the staff through informal discussions about her family and was encouraged to attend various conferences and workshops. That is when her journey took a sharp turn:

> I was knee deep in denial. My mother definitely is narcissistic. I was born and raised to look after her, fulfill her comfort needs, emotionally and materially—to put her first before myself, before others, my children, especially men. I had such poor self-esteem, I would wait for others' approval, never, ever taking a risk. If I heard one negative comment about myself, it would send me crashing into a deeper depression for days. My mother would pooh-pooh my concerns, my sadness. She was the focus; I was her handmaiden. She craftily placed a wedge between her two daughters, my sister, now age forty-three, and my father. She kept him at a distance, always juggling, maneuvering us like pawns on a chessboard.

No one spoke in our family, unless it was my mother.
I guess I would have been more aware of her deviousness
if she had been a screamer or abused us physically. However, every word, every look, every phrase was carefully
planned out beforehand and stated matter of factly. This
gave her great control and omnipotence.

Beth describes herself as "terribly shy," spending much of her early
and adolescent years in her room, reading, and feeling more and
more depressed. She writes that her mother never encouraged her
academically or socially. Now, she says, "I do not like this woman,
my mother. I have searched my soul and heart, and I cannot find
one redeeming quality that exists in this woman. She has always
been a thorn in my side and will continue to be so until she dies.
Then I will be released."

Turning the Corner

Beth's anger keeps her a Wandering Daughter. It is when we daughters are able to place our mothers in context that we take the turn
back to her. Consider that Beth's mother was the daughter of immigrants, and according to Beth, "My mother and her sisters were
taught whatever was significant and important for survival during
the early 1920s." Beth does not elaborate on what these survival
skills were.

She describes her mother as a woman who "never stopped. She
would make plans to go out constantly when she wasn't working
(usually visiting her mother—seeking acceptance)." She was married to a man who worked very sporadically. "My father never really
worked much after his illness. He had been a purchasing agent—
belligerent, angry, always being let go [fired] because of his inability to get along with others." From 1961 until his death in 1984, he
suffered from severe depression, had multiple strokes, was wheel-
chair bound, and was in and out of hospitals. Beth's mother had to
become the breadwinner and take responsibility for the family.

Reading between the lines, it is clear that although Beth was not close to her father and he abused her, she had some compassion for him, especially since he had to live with her mother. Although Beth's father physically abused her, she seems to blame her mother for not protecting her. Based on the information she shared, we could assume that perhaps Beth's inability to demonstrate some compassion for her mother may have to do with viewing her mother through the cultural lens of the idealized mother. It might help if she were to learn more about both the era in which her mother lived and her mother's early background, particularly from the perspective of her mother's friends or from aunts and uncles.

Given our research and what other respondents have been able to appreciate in their mothers, we discovered some small gifts that Beth's mother has passed along to her, although she stands too far away to notice them. One particular gift, and one that seems to have been a mantra of mothers to baby boomer daughters, is, "Finish your education; go to college; make sure you have something to fall back on, just in case." Beth's mother is no exception, although Beth's slant on her message is influenced by her anger toward her mom: "My mother always told me to take typing and business courses as it will give you something to 'fall back on' when your husband leaves you."

Perhaps someday, Beth will be able to see the wisdom embedded deep within the message.

A Surprising Transformation

Renee, a married, forty-two-year-old physician and mother of two, is a striking example of how a Wandering Daughter can suddenly, and quite unexpectedly, take the turn back home.

Renee was one of five women we asked to participate in a group discussion in Cincinnati. It appeared from her survey responses as though she still had a somewhat painful relationship with her mom, a recent widow who had been a homemaker most of her life, with a few occasional part-time jobs during marriage, "usually in factories, limited to six months or less." Renee's dad was a skilled laborer and had had his own business for about twelve years, followed by a full-time position within a public school system.

The oldest of three, Renee, a very attractive, gentle, and soft-spoken woman, talks about her adolescent years: "I got married after high school and got divorced about four years later. I got married strictly to get away from my mother, and I was a telephone receptionist for a couple of years before deciding to go to college. We all ended up doing that, but without any encouragement from home, so I think it was a matter of self-survival. You just realized that there was a hole in your soul, and you struggled until you could find it."

In describing her mom, Renee says sadly, "She was really a pretty angry and bitter woman most of my growing-up years. And most of what I know about her life was that her mother was an alcoholic, and there was physical abuse in the family. And I know that when she worked right after she got out of high school, her mother would take her money to go to the bars and drink." Renee remembers hearing how much fun her mom had when she was single and working before she had a husband and kids:

> She talked about the wonderful, beautiful clothes she could buy, and the car she owned, and the figure she had, and on and on and on. And then the next breath was how she didn't have any of those things now. She didn't work when we were growing up, and I remember during this time thinking, "This woman should be working. This woman should have a career. She is not happy doing what she's doing." And my mother is still that way. I've tried to come to grips now with where she is and to try to understand her, but it's difficult; it's really difficult because the negativity persists. There are always barbs and manipulative kinds of comments.

As the group session progressed, several times when we asked specific questions, Renee, with some discomfort, would say, "I'm not ready to answer that yet. I don't know the answer," or "I don't know how to answer that one."

Although Renee's mom did not encourage higher education and in fact discouraged it for her daughters, her big push for Renee's brother was to make sure he got a job with good benefits. But for the girls she advised, "'Find somebody that will take care of you. Make sure they have a good job with good benefits.' Benefits were high on my mother's priority list."

With great sadness, Renee says, "I would wish for a different mother. It goes back so far that I can't even begin to think of how I would've changed the relationship other than to ask for a different mother. And I keep in touch with her a lot still, but I realize that a lot of it is just out of a sense of duty and guilt and all those things. My father died a couple of years ago and clearly, he was my favorite parent."

As the group discussion progressed, another group member, Celia, a Prodigal Daughter, forty-one, married, and a homemaker with four children ranging in age from seven to fifteen, began talking about what she has realized her mother is right about. Celia was the oldest girl of seven children:

> I think my sisters and I were quite romantic. Well, I should say the first three sisters; the younger two were much more interested in finding a rich guy. But the older three were much more romantic in our outlook. And my mom would say, "You know, love is fine and dandy, but you've got to have money to live." And I would think, "Oh, mother, you are so crass! I can't believe you are saying that." But I have come to realize it really is hard to live without money.

As though a light bulb had gone off, Renee, with a smile on her face, blurted out, "I'm just beginning to realize how important it is to have benefits—you know, health insurance, pensions plans!" The group howled with laughter. Somehow, intermingled with this laughter, there seemed to be a sense of joy within the group that Renee was able to discover something worthwhile in her relationship with her mom.

The most dramatic turn came at the very end of our session when members were talking about how they have come to value their mothers, particularly as women. Renee's insights poignantly spoke to what we all felt deep inside:

> Even though I don't like some of the qualities about her, I do see that she is a pretty tough nut, and I suppose in that sense I admire that part of her. Clearly, she is a real survivor; she likes to take care of herself and prides herself on that ability, even though she has been just a housewife all these years. She's pretty strong.

In spite of the hurt and disappointment, Renee may be taking the trip back.

You Can Go Home Again

Counseling, which many of the survey respondents indicated has helped them gain a different perspective on their relationship with their mothers, can be particularly helpful to the Wandering Daughter. Women's discussion groups, such as the one we had, or just plain old-fashioned coffee klatsches or dinner clubs, can also help to alter and crystallize a woman's take on her mom. We can use our strength as women and our natural ability to connect, empathize, and share with each other to continue to expand our view of our mothers. It is most helpful to keep these conversations positive. Rather than focusing on what our moms have done wrong, we need to reflect more on what they have done right.

Although therapy can help in a more formal way, the traditional kind tends to focus on the "not-good-enough" mothering dished out by our moms. It tends to fuel our anger by dwelling on their failures.

Interestingly enough, if a woman speaks positively of her mother, clinicians inwardly note, "Idealization," and interpret this as further signs of dependency and enmeshment! God forbid we should idealize our mothers and think highly of them. With the advent of managed care, what is now termed "solution-based treatment"—helping people look at what is going well within our primary relationships and the resiliencies and strengths gained from these—is becoming more the norm.

The Prodigal Daughter

The Prodigal Daughter–mother relationship is characterized by the typical adolescent rebellion (although some may be more tumultuous than the average), followed by an ongoing distant, sometimes tense relationship with waves of anger, resentment, and guilt thrashing about. For a large portion of her adult life, the daughter generally has rejected many of her mother's ideas, opinions, or lifestyle choices, at least until midlife. Then she begins to see her mother more as a person in her own right, a woman with a past, as both a daughter and a female influenced by the culture in which she grew up. The emotional markers of this relationship are compassion, sadness, joy, peace, humor, and acceptance. These women have typically refashioned their relationship with their mothers so that it is more reciprocal, or at least less conflicted. Daughters are more able to set appropriate limits with their mothers by being assertive or, through the power of choice, are able to let things go or even agree to disagree with their mothers when a difference arises. For the most part, these daughters follow the rule of the old saying: Choose your battles wisely.

Cruising with Mom

Jo, a forty-four-year old divorced mother of two, not only completed our survey but also participated in our group discussion. An outgoing, attractive, and verbal woman, Jo, who holds an M.B.A. and is an executive director of a housing agency, has always worked within the social services field. She was the third of six children, one of two girls. Her mom, now age sixty-seven, first worked outside the home after divorcing Jo's father, who was in educational administration; she was employed as a lab technician and sickle cell counselor for the Veterans Hospital until her retirement.

Jo epitomizes the Prodigal Daughter. In her survey, Jo says, "I probably discounted everything my mother said. I plain did not like her!" Yet now she values her as a "person, mother, and friend." She says it was at the time of her first pregnancy that she began to realize the love and concern her mom had for her, and it was with this event that she started her journey back.

Interestingly enough, during some actual trips with her mother, she began to experience another dimension of this relationship and began to mellow. In her strikingly resonant and animated voice, Jo says, "I've just come back from a vacation with my mom: a ten-day cruise to Alaska. And it was wonderful. But I couldn't have done it ten years ago, and definitely not fifteen years ago. My sister, my mother, and I went to Alaska because she said she wanted to do it, and we just kind of went [rolling her eyes], 'Uh huh.' We really didn't want to go to Alaska, and none of her friends wanted to go to Alaska." Jo laughs as she reminisces about the trip and how she and her sister took turns staying up until midnight taking their mother to the midnight buffet, the event her mom most enjoyed and looked forward to on the trip. Her voice drops as she sadly says, "My mother is ill now. That trip will probably be one of the things that I'm going to always be very glad that I did. And probably I'm going to think that I wish we would've had a better relationship earlier so that we could've done more of these types of things."

During this discussion, Renee, still in her Wandering Daughter mode, talked about a cruise she took with her family and her mother that was very stressful: "Since I sent in that survey, I was on vacation with her for a week, and it was just … just very difficult. You know, all the old feelings came back as to why I left home when

I did and why I'm not living in the same town with her and all of these things."

Jo did not miss a beat: "We took my mother to the Bahamas two years ago to see if we could do it. So we figured we ought to try something small first—just three days. And when it was over, we thought it wasn't all that bad and maybe we should've tried for five days. Well, I came to my senses and said, 'No, let's not push it. Let's work up to it.' And we did. We worked up to the ten-day Alaska trip that way."

Renee laughs as she says, "That was my mistake! I spent a week with my mom!" We all agreed that regardless of the quality of our relationships with our mothers, short trips seem to be the place to start when traveling together!

Issues of Neglect and Abuse

Prodigal Daughters are not immune from having received verbal and physical abuse at the hands of their moms, as with Miranda, a forty-eight-year-old, divorced, full-time elementary school librarian. Her mother is seventy-eight, has been married fifty-seven years, graduated from high school, and has never worked outside the home. Of her mother, Miranda says, "I've always known she was bright, as well as shrewd, and possessed a great deal of common sense. She's always maintained she only made one mistake in her life: once she thought she was wrong, but she was really right!"

As a teenager, Miranda developed a better understanding of her mom's unpredictable and verbally abusive behavior when she first realized her mom was an alcoholic:

> When she's sober, she's my best friend, and I can always
> count on her. When she's drinking, I don't want to see,
> hear, or talk to her; I don't want to be around her, nor do
> I want my friends subjected to it. She's unreliable when
> she drinks, and now [because she's elderly] I worry much
> more about her—and my dad—especially when they're

in Michigan for six months of the year. I always love her, but I don't always love what she does. I resent all the time and opportunities we've lost because of her alcoholism.

My self-confidence has suffered because of my mother. All my life I've seen her do anything she wanted to do, anytime she wanted to do it. There's nothing that's been beyond her reach or her ability. I'm not as accomplished as I'd like to be in many areas; I know it, and I accept my limitations—although it's frustrating. When my mother is under the influence of alcohol, she has an extremely caustic tongue. I've always been sensitive, and she has many times verbally chewed me up and spit me out. She doesn't do it now, because I'm onto her, and she knows it. I speak my mind to her now, and I no longer am intimidated by her as I was when I was younger.

In writing about her grandmother's death, Miranda experienced a deep connection with her mother, which she poignantly describes:

When my grandmother died, my mother said to me, "You only have one mother." I was embracing my mom and telling her how sorry I was [about the loss of her mother]; she was crying—which I don't think I've seen her do more than five times in my entire life. I've often thought how true that statement is, and when she passes away, I'll be devastated. In spite of her faults, she's always been behind me when I really needed help and support—and I can't imagine my life without her. I've always said she's like the little girl with the curl. There was a little girl who had a little curl right in the middle of her forehead. When she was good, she was very, very good. But when she was bad, she was horrid! One either loves her or hates her, but she's certainly never been boring. Nor would I have ever gone through with trading her in for a new model!

Some Prodigal Daughters even experienced sexual abuse from dads and stepdads, as in the case of Jean Marie, a forty-two-year-old divorced mother of two who has some college and is currently working in the emergency room of a midwestern hospital. Her mother, a high school graduate who is sixty-three and disabled, worked as a cashier and bookkeeper.

She reports that she did not get along with her mother as a teenager and says, "It was her way or no way. I was afraid to speak out. I saw that she cared for others more than she did me." As the oldest of five girls, Jean Marie says, "I took care of all of us. My stepfather abused me and my sister sexually, and all of us, including my mom, physically and emotionally. She allowed the abuse and wasn't strong enough to leave, yet she showed the world we had a perfect family. She now has lung cancer. She is still blaming others and is always negative about life and people and put out about something. She is sick, and I feel sorry for her but will not take on her pain. Mostly I feel sorry and pity her."

Jean Marie continues, "I've been in therapy forever and now can live a healthy life, not that of a victim. I realize she did the best she could with what knowledge and strength she had. I accept that she allowed things to happen to me, sexually and physically, and she is dying because she holds that in."

In spite of some real neglect and abuse, these women have been able to develop compassion and understanding for their mothers by seeing them as women—people with human limitations. Prodigal Daughters are able to take the "m" out of *mother* and truly see her as an "other."

The Untraveled Daughter

The Untraveled Daughter–mother relationship is characterized by typical adolescent rebellion—possibly dramatic or relatively benign—but then is followed by a deeper reconnection. The relation-ship is a close one in which feelings are shared, though our generation would still quantify the level of sharing as more superficial than deep. These women are likely to say that their mothers think their daugh-ters are more open than they actually are. This daughter tends to be protective of her mom and keeps any thought, feeling, or opinion that could potentially hurt or displease her a secret unto herself. The emo-tional markers of this relationship are similar to those of the Prodigal Daughter: compassion, joy, peace, humor, sadness, and respect.

The Good-Enough Mother

Some Untraveled Daughters take great pride in being just like their mothers. Thirty-nine-year-old Sara, single and the oldest of five chil-dren, is one of them: "When I was a child, I always knew I was like my mother. I always wanted to be around her and see what she was doing and why." When she was a teenager, she and her mother were best friends and rarely disagreed, which she says continues to this day.

When asked if there is anything about her mother she may have discounted, she says, "Nothing. I value, respect, and honor every-thing she ever gave me. My mother and I have a wonderful rela-tionship. I can talk to my mother about anything and never have to feel embarrassed. She is a wonderful woman. I don't know what I would do if anything happens to her, and when she dies, I know my life will suffer a void that no one or no thing can ever replace. My mother is a very special and wonderful person. She is a saint."

Another of our respondents, a thirty-five-year-old single comp-troller, the youngest of five, says:

> My mother taught through example. She's educated, poised, witty, well spoken, and polite. At times she seems almost meek, yet I know her convictions are as strong as mine. I tend to talk until there are no words left unsaid. She says precisely the correct amount to get her point across. Through consistency in behavior, I

now understand the amount of patience she must have, to put up with my spinning like a top! My mother is the steady rock in my life. Through everything, she has always been there for me, sometimes quietly. My greatest gift to her would be for me to be happy in my life. What would make me happy is if I thought she saw me as a constant friend and companion. I will always be there for her, probably sometimes quietly, but always.

Untraveled Daughters often report that their relationships with their moms are unmarked by any conflicts, as in the case of Maggie, a forty-four-year-old single realtor: "We never didn't get along, but the love has grown and developed. We are very different in lifestyle, likes, and dislikes. But I'm proud to share her sense of humor, responsibility, and love of family values—though it may seem strange that a daughter isn't able to recall any motherly traumas. I think it's an old wives' tale that friction is a necessary ingredient in all mother-daughter relationships. My mom and I would make boring guests on the screaming talk shows. We laugh together, cry together, hope together, and rejoice together. She is my best friend, and I hope that I am one of hers.

Far from Perfect

Untraveled Daughters do not necessarily have moms who led ideal, traditional lives. Angela is a fifty-one-year-old widow with three daughters. Her mother, married and divorced three times, is seventy-four and the mother of three, with Angela being the middle child. Angela's mother did not finish high school, but was very talented and artistic, and she generally worked in jobs that were connected to her husbands' careers.

In talking about her early teenage years with her mother, Angela says, "My mother was gone a great deal, as she traveled to get away from her bad marriages. But despite her absences, I always knew she loved me tremendously. My mother never talked much about us or what she wanted for us. Her main thrust was to find the one true love who would make her life complete. I always hoped she would have this love. However, she never did. My mother and I rarely spoke of things that interested me. She was and is very self-centered, but I always knew she loved us deeply."

Angela does not report any turn away from her mom; she evinces no real anger at what other daughters might have resented, like her mom's absences and self-centeredness. As an Untraveled Daughter, Angela has been able to keep her mother's positive qualities, which eclipse her deficiencies, in the forefront. Further, she has been able to discern the gifts her mother was capable of giving: "For the times, my mother took big risks to better our lives. She was subjected to ridicule due to divorces, but she maintained style and grace and strove to get us all in secure situations. She was a great deal like 'Auntie Mame,' and I admired her. I had a wonderful if somewhat lonely childhood, but it was exciting and always an adventure."

We do not judge these categories for what goes on in the mother-daughter relationship as better or worse than the other. Instead, we think the relationship with our mothers is an ongoing, ever-changing process. We are moved along in our individual journeys by our own internal readiness to face the reality of our mothers and of ourselves. Midlife just gives us a nudge, for some of us maybe even a shove.

Before we discuss the gifts our moms passed down to us and the ways in which they most influenced us, we will take a step back into time and examine those sociocultural factors that shaped not only our mothers' lives but ours as well as we came of age.

The Way They Were

*You know the trouble with women is—they ask just
too many questions. They should spend all their time
just being beautiful.*

Humphrey Bogart, Dead Reckoning (1947)

In 1946, the world of our mothers was turbulent and uncertain. A
world war had just claimed the lives of 292,131 Americans and
42,000 Canadians. The Vatican estimated that civilian and military casualties totaled 22 million. That same year, when millions of
baby girls started arriving in maternity wards in record numbers
from Missoula to Montreal, these young mothers also faced the
challenge of putting their lives back together again after the war.
These women were beginning married life still scraping by on
rationing coupons, and at the same time they were learning how to
relate to a man whose wartime experiences were something he
could barely talk about. If our mothers had had jobs in what had
been labeled "men's work," taking the place of GIs overseas, they
were either laid off or fired when Johnny Came Marching Home,
or they were strenuously encouraged to get out of the factory and
back in the kitchen.

What was the news on page one that year? The Nuremberg war
crimes trials had begun; Hermann Göring and eleven other Nazi
chiefs were sentenced to death for atrocities they had committed

during World War II. *Life* magazine featured a bizarre photo collage of Prince Fumimara Konoye of Japan in repose. He had killed himself rather than face a war crimes trial but had issued invitations to his family, friends, and colleagues before poisoning himself, so they could bid him adieu.

The outlines of the unfathomable Holocaust were beginning to emerge. News about death camps, concentration camps, and slave labor camps was beginning to filter down to the popular press. In Europe, 25 million people were homeless, and in Warsaw, 1 million people had no homes and lived in holes in the ground. According to *Life* magazine, "the first winter of peace holds Europe in a deathly grip of cold, hunger and hopelessness."

At home, despite the return of our mother's husbands and boyfriends, difficulties flourished. A gallon of milk cost nearly as much as the hourly minimum wage of seventy-five cents. Our mothers still had to cope with ration coupons, and they had another year of sugar rationing to go. Yet the great emphasis was placed on our mothers' creating a happy home—just like in the movies and in the pages of *Life* and *Ladies' Home Journal*. The difficulties of postwar adjustment were rarely dealt with openly in those sources or in films. Hollywood, for one, is credited with few realistic forays into the world of the returning vets, and only the Academy Award–winning film *The Best Years of Our Lives*, starring Dana Andrews and Myrna Loy, depicted a less-than-perfect situation. Here, the trials of three World War II veterans and their wives in attempting to put the war behind them and begin anew were treated sensitively and realistically. (One of the actors, Harold Russell, in fact was a returning veteran.)

The Best Birth Control Is an Aspirin Between Your Knees

Our mothers' control over their reproductive lives was, by today's standards, archaic. In the 1940s, condoms and douching represented 72 percent of all birth control, with diaphragms and jelly just 7 percent of use. By 1955, a study indicated that 43 percent of the time, women were still relying on their partner to use a condom; 34 percent tried the rhythm method; 37 percent used a diaphragm; and 15 percent were still banking on withdrawal. Bernard Asbell, in his history of the birth control pill, cites a 1951 book, *Planned Parenthood: A Practical Guide to Birth Control Methods*, which looked at Lysol as a birth control measure used by women who were treated at a Newark, New Jersey, mental health center. Lysol, used as a douche, could bring on an "overdue period"; it worked like a sort of rough "morning after" liquid pill. Of 507 users, 250 got pregnant, so the authors deduced that lemon juice or vinegar were better spermicides. Additionally, cervical pessaries—or "womb veils" in the shape of a wishbone—and rings were also inserted into the cervical canal and used for contraception. In a 1947 article in the *American Journal of Obstetrics and Gynecology*, author Dr. Leon Israel reported on a number of cases of pelvic inflammation and a dozen critical cases of peritonitis because women were using these wishbone-shaped pessaries. Seventeen states still had laws limiting the sale, distribution, and advertising of contraception.

There were hundreds of feminine hygiene products, most of them relatively useless. One, a powder, had to be blown into the vagina with what Asbell says was an "instrument resembling a bazooka." Another, called "Zonite," was a douche whose ads showed a teary young wife wondering why her husband has turned away from her. "Why are his kisses just pecks now?" she wonders.

Then there was That Time of the Month. Bulky sanitary napkins with safety pins were still the most widely used product for menstruation, although this was still an advance on rags, which many women had to make do with during the Depression and the war. In a 1946 ad for Modess sanitary napkins in *Life* magazine, three young women are shown commiserating about the problem: "Gosh, how I used to stew and fret about offending at times like this!" says one. Her friend replies that "it used to haunt me too—till Modess with deodorant came along!"

In the world of our mothers, a pre–Masters and Johnson world, advice about sex could be thought worthwhile and credible even when handed out by the former first lady, Eleanor Roosevelt, in the pages of *Ladies' Home Journal* (subtitled *The Magazine Women Believe In*). Mrs. Roosevelt answered questions about some weighty issues— for example, whether readers were likely to see World War III—but she also responded to questions about subjects such as "necking and petting." She wrote, "A girl is wise if she does not make herself cheap. . . . A really nice young man would understand quite well that until a girl is really attracted to him, she did not care to be mauled." If Mrs. Roosevelt could hand out information with credibility, certainly doctors were considered wise, and their counsel was followed. It may seem unbelievable now, but *Ladies' Home Journal* ran ads proclaiming, "More Doctors Smoke Camels Than Any Other Cigarette." Old Gold cigarette ads urged a young woman to offer her husband a cigarette. That would help control his temper as he wrestled with putting chains on his tires during a snowstorm.

Is There a Ford in Your Future?

Mom may have been struggling to make ends meet and relying on plenty of Spam and other versions (and there were several) of cheap meat products to stretch her grocery budget, but the popular media began breathlessly to advertise the virtues of the "good life" that awaited any family, in the form of new, shiny cars, home ownership, and labor-saving devices. Most baby boomer daughters born in the late 1940s remember that mom had *no* dishwasher or dryer and that dishes had to be washed and dried by hand. If the children helped— and they often did—this could regularly be the cause of quarrels between sisters and brothers as to the quality of the final "product." Sometimes it seemed easier for mom just to do the darn dishes herself. (*But*, mom had to beware dishpan hands. Lux detergent ran ads showing how a young wife disgraced her husband in front of his boss when he brought the old guy home for dinner. Why? She had dishpan hands.) As for dryers, few homes had one. Instead, mom (and sometimes her daughter) hung the wet clothes on the clothesline. In the winter, they froze stiff as boards and had to be folded awkwardly and wrestled into shape.

Everything Is Copasetic

Mom may have been Rosie the Riveter or she may have gone to college (or both), but after the war, all the forces conspired to get her back to where she belonged: in the home. When the U.S. and Canadian governments offered GIs cheap tuition and board, men flocked to universities. Hollywood played a major role in this conversion to peacetime activities. Despite the genre of the "woman's film," which depicted bright, sassy, adventurous, glamorous, and opinionated women in the 1930s and 1940s, film historians such as Jeanine Basinger and Molly Haskell argue that women in these films may have simply stepped outside the rules and been free for part of the plot, but they had to die for their sins or live a much-reduced kind of existence at the end. Importantly, women in these films were *always* destined to come back home. Says Basinger, "The woman's film was successful because it worked out of a paradox. It both held women in social bondage and released them into a dream of potency and freedom. It drew women in with images of what was lacking in their own lives and sent them home reassured that their own lives were the right thing after all. . . . To convince women that marriage and motherhood were the right path, movies had to show women making the mistake of doing something else." Or, as Rosalind Russell argued in the 1935 flick *Rendezvous*, "It's a man's place to make the money for the house and the woman's place to take care of the man when he comes home. A woman with a career wouldn't have time to bring up a lot of kids."

Basinger cites the Loretta Young and Geraldine Fitzgerald 1944 World War I film *Ladies Courageous*, where the heroines leave home, learn to fly, risk their lives ferrying bombers during World

War II, and are seen as doing a good job. But like all other films showing women doing men's work, this is seen as unusual, and the happy ending is to marry, like Fitzgerald, not "go free . . . make a path through the sky . . . mark no trail," as Young argues that she dreams of doing. She is killed in action; Fitzgerald marries and lives happily ever after.

Like Loretta Young, American and Canadian women really did pitch in during the war. It was not just a celluloid fantasy. In fact, Bureau of the Census figures show that women's participation in the U.S. workforce rose from 27 percent at the beginning of the war to 35 percent. And nearly 60 percent of single women were working by 1944, according to the bureau.

This was the experience of the mothers of our respondents. The vast majority of these women worked during the war: in ammunition plants, in steel foundries, as WAVEs, as switchboard operators, as Big Band music singers. Typical is Marilyn, an office manager from Cincinnati, whose seventy-four-year-old mom worked "in an antiaircraft gun factory in the 1940s, grinding lenses for gun sights. Then she was a singer for a Big Band in the 1940s. She married at twenty-three, became a housewife, and had eight kids."

Having kids and staying home was where the Powers That Be determined women belonged. Even that enlightened leader, Adlai Stevenson, promoted the idea that no matter how much money and time and energy may have been spent on getting an education, women belonged at home. In an address to the graduates of Smith College in 1955 (a class that included his future daughter-in-law), Stevenson maintained that there was a historical crisis at work involving totalitarianism, but that nonetheless there was much that Smith graduates could do "in the humble role of housewife—which, statistically, is what most of you are going to be whether you like the idea or not just now—and you'll like it!"

While attempting to sell the idea of gentle persuasion of men-folk, Stevenson argued that nowadays the young wife or mother is short of time . . . and that, once immersed in the pressing problems of domesticity, many women feel frustrated and far apart from the great issues and stirring debates for which their education has given them understanding and relish. Once they read Baudelaire. Now it is the *Consumer's Guide*. Once they wrote poetry. Now, the laundry list. Once they discussed art and philosophy until late in the night. Now, they are so tired they fall asleep as soon as the dishes are finished. There is, often, a sense of contraction, of closing horizons and lost opportunities. They had hoped to play their part in the crisis of the age. But what they do is wash the diapers.

In a 1948 survey of its members, the *Journal of the American Association of University Women* reported that 45 percent of university graduates listed themselves as having no occupation. Half also listed themselves as mothers. The AAUW, unlike Stevenson, did not think this was the best way to take advantage of women's skills and urged President Harry Truman to appoint women to policymaking jobs and strike a commission to figure out how to "profit" from all the war work women had done. For those women who *were* in the workforce, the organization argued for better job conditions and flexible work hours for married women, especially those with children.

Ladies' Home Journal, however, kept up a steady drumbeat for mothers at home. Baby boomer daughters often complain about the unrealistic expectations everyone has of them and their multiple responsibilities. But according to popular culture in the 1940s and 1950s, our mothers should have been carving out an Eden at home, with well-behaved, well-dressed children, meals that would have taken hours to make in a pre-microwave, pre-prepackaged food, pre-McDonald's world. They would have a beatific smile on their faces. Ads for sparkling dishes, thanks to Lux, were presided over by women in elaborate hair styles, two-inch heels, and hose. And no matter how interesting a career "gal" might seem, she too only wished for a husband and kids at the end of the day, according to *Ladies' Home Journal*. Following three carefree roommates who lived in Manhattan and who seemed to be having quite a good life, the magazine quoted one of them named Gretchen, who made $177 a week at American Express, a job that she viewed as only temporary. Did she want "a career for life"? No, she replied. Rather, what she wanted was "to do a cracking good job of raising a family!"

Then there was the cautionary tale of Minnesota Congresswoman Coya Knutson, which made headlines around the country. Although women had been in Congress continuously for thirty years, Mr. Knutson launched an attack on his wife for having deserted "the happy home we once enjoyed." Although he was a drunk and the home was decidedly not happy, the resulting publicity painted Mrs. Knutson as an uncaring woman who had abandoned her family for life in Washington's fast lane. In spite of her legislative firsts—the first House appropriations for cystic fibrosis, the first bill calling for income tax checkoffs to finance presidential elections, and legislation establishing student loans—she was defeated in 1958. Film critic Molly Haskell argues that Hollywood agreed with Mr. Knutson and had created a "circumscribed world of the housewife [that] corresponds to the state of woman in general, confronted by a range of options so limited she might as well inhabit a cell." Or, as Jeanine Basinger puts it, Hollywood saw "marriage as the ultimate solution. . . . The proper behavior for a woman: keep busy in marriage, serve her husband's career, take care of her family and stay at home. Then, the marriage will flourish."

Not Exactly Like *The Donna Reed Show*

Even though *Life*, *Ladies' Home Journal*, *Saturday Evening Post*, Hollywood, and just about everyone thought our mothers should stay at home, our respondents' mothers turned out to have had to work anyway. Only 43 out of 160 of our respondents described their mothers solely as homemakers.

When our survey moms went back into the workforce, it was usually when her children were adolescents. In other cases, mothers went back and forth, in and out of the workforce to make ends meet, regardless. Billie, who listed herself as a waitress–dress designer, is typical: "As far as I know, my mother became an R.N. in 1953—and she worked until she got married in 1957, had me in 1958, and then I think she went back to work part-time in a hospital in the late 1960s. She did that for awhile and then worked in several bookstores in the 1970s, went back to nursing in the late 1970s and 1980s. Now, she's stuck almost twenty-four hours a day taking care of my father, formerly a golf professional, now severely disabled and practically a vegetable."

A computer programmer from Texas describes her sixty-seven-year-old mother's teaching career and homemaking like this: "To the best of my knowledge, my mother taught from her graduation from college—I think it was 1945—until my birth in 1955. She resumed teaching when my sister turned six in 1966. She worked the majority of that time as a secondary-level teacher with the Waco Independent Schools. But she'd also worked in an ammunitions plant during World War II."

Our mothers were often forced into the workplace because of divorce and lax child-support laws and enforcement. Ellie, a culinary consultant from Chicago, remembers that when her parents divorced in the 1950s, even though both were "Old World Thinking" (her mother was from Russia, her dad from Silesia), Ellie's mom had to find a job to support herself and her daughter. She spent the next "thirty-six years pounding on a typewriter" at a Veterans Administration hospital in suburban Detroit.

Even if everything had gone according to the Grand Plan and women had stayed at home during their childbearing years, once those kids had left the home, respected icons of advice such as Eleanor Roosevelt still believed that women's prime function was "to meet the needs of those who are nearest and dearest to her," which meant that she would have to find things to do but, once again, stay put in the home. Still, the former first lady did agree that women ought to have some outside interests, so they would not be a drag on everyone else in the family. As she put it, "It is important that young families should never have the feeling that the older members of the family are languishing for their constant companionship. This makes the time they spend together less enjoyable." This might be considered a difficult feat if mom had followed Eleanor's advice and stayed close to the hearth!

Nevertheless, the career pattern of our mothers, as described by our respondents, was not entirely what Eleanor Roosevelt could have imagined. Theirs is a crazy quilt of traditional and nontraditional jobs, jobs they took during the war to help out and jobs they took after it to supplement (or in some cases totally support) their families' incomes. In addition to their wartime work, our respondents' mothers walked out the front door and earned a paycheck when their kids were still at home. They were everything from waitresses to maids, cooks in the school cafeteria, food checkers, cheese checkers, jewel checkers, Avon ladies, travel agents, piano teachers, cleaning ladies, barmaids, assistants in bakeries, IRS workers, librarians, seamstresses, cinema attendants, cashiers, florists, shelve stockers, sewing machine saleswomen, child care workers. A few mothers were professionals, apart from the nursing and teaching fields. Some worked for magazines, one was a university president, one a model, one a fashion illustrator, another a sickle cell counselor at a hospital.

Often the careers of our survey mothers were as elaborately stitched together as any quilt they might have made for our beds. This part of their lives is something we have not really thought about. Rather, the conventional wisdom is that our mothers' generation were stay-at-home, *Donna Reed* moms. At least for our respondents, they were much more than that.

Stop, Hey, What's That Sound, Everybody Look What's Going Down

In 1946, the year many of our moms were learning what peacetime would mean to them and getting to know our fathers again after their absence overseas, the same year that the Nuremberg Trials began and the U.S. Senate killed the Equal Rights Amendment, the year that Oldsmobile introduced its new Hydramatic drive ("the new style in Postwar Driving"), 1,359,499 baby girls were born in the United States. Nobody took these "extra" births in 1946 as the great event they would herald. In fact, as Landon Y. Jones argues in *Great Expectations: America and the Baby Boom Generation*, demographers were unimpressed: "The rise in births was sudden, they agreed, but surely it was little other than a freakish postwar adjustment, a classic case of satisfying pent-up demand." Even so, 20 percent more babies had been born in the United States in 1946 than in 1945. We thus arrived in overcrowded maternity wards, whose personnel were unprepared for our numbers, and we proceeded on to kindergarten, grade school, junior high, high school, and college. Each time there were always more of us than ever before. By the time someone had labeled us the "baby boom," our numbers had changed the landscape of North America forever. We would transform the way suburbia looked, the way education was delivered, the kind of music and popular culture that was consumed, and politics (eighteen-year-olds got the vote in 1972). Much of what we surveyed we began to change—whether we meant to or not.

When the first baby boomer girls graduated from college in 1967 the world had become a much more disturbed place than the placid and bucolic world many of us inhabited during our childhood. *Time* magazine, in a cover story called "To Heal a Nation," diagnosed the United States in 1968 "as if verging on a national nervous breakdown." Vietnam, a place few of us had learned about in geography class and almost eighty-five hundred miles away, mired the United

States in a terrible war it had assumed it would win, but it could not. "The Reds" kept finding ways of winning battles. *Time* featured the story of a graduate of Jesuit-run Le Moyne College who burned his draft card, calling "napalming immoral." Martin Luther King, Jr., and Bobby Kennedy were assassinated in 1968, and segregationist George Wallace was making a serious run for the presidency. Columbia University nearly fell to students, who were protesting their lack of input into the curriculum, and the Democratic National Convention in Chicago shamed itself and its host city when police clubbed protesters for television viewers in North America to see.

Hey There, Georgy Girl, Why Do All the Boys Just Pass You By?

In a strange contrast to the celluloid fantasies created for our mothers' collective enjoyment, Hollywood gave baby boomer daughters in the 1960s and 1970s little in the way of strong women role models. In fact, argues Molly Haskell, the American film's view of woman became decidedly chauvinistic. With the breakup of the studio system and the rise of the male film director, she argues, women in film became what the male director fantasized she should be: a pin-up girl, "an ingenue, a mail-order cover girl. . . . In every case, we got not only less than we might have expected and hoped for, but less than ever before: women who were less intelligent, less sensual, less humorous, and altogether less extraordinary than the women in the twenties, the thirties, the forties, or even the poor, pallid, uptight fifties." And now those two strong women icons of "the woman's film," Joan Crawford and Bette Davis, were turned into transvestites in *What Ever Happened to Baby Jane?* Thank goodness for television's Emma Peel, the bright, beautiful sleuth in *The Avengers*, the British series imported to North America in the 1960s. Emma was equal to John Steed, her partner; she could figure out abstruse clues, and she could also level the bad guys with one judo chop. And she wasn't considered a lesbian or a man-hating witch. But she had little company in the way of role models for young baby boomer girls on television or in films. The creators of television's *Gidget* eliminated the problem of a teenage girl's relating to a mother during adolescence: Gidget's mother was dead. (Of course, there was the intrepid teenage sleuth, Nancy Drew, confined to the pages of a series of books. Still, she was clearly more clever than her boyfriend, Ned. Like Gidget, she did not have to deal with a mother because she too was motherless.)

Here we were, baby boomer women coming out of universities in record numbers, educated to do something important—more important than typing up our boyfriends' term papers—faced with images in magazines and television and movies that gave us role models like Raquel Welch or Jane Fonda as Barbarella.

When we became active in the antiwar movement and in other political campaigns in the late 1960s in both Canada and the United States, we were still doing the typing and fetching the coffee (or the marijuana). There were few leaders among us, and we still seemed to be the handmaidens of men, as our mothers had been before us. We worked for John Lindsay when he ran for New York City mayor; Senator Eugene McCarthy and Bobby Kennedy, when they ran for president of the United States; and Pierre Trudeau when he ran for prime minister in Canada—but we were not running these campaigns. Even when we undertook serious business in politics, mainstream media like *Time* would still insist on describing how we looked as much as what we had to say. In 1968, a University of California coed and a member of the Communist Party refused to register as such as required by the McCarran Act of the 1950s and thus was liable for fines of $12,000 as well as over five thousand years in jail. She challenged the act and took her fight to the U.S. Supreme Court. When she won, this is how *Time* described her:

"Yippee!" shouted the petite Berkeley coed, her braid flying as she leaped into the air. For [this coed], 21, a junior
studying history at the University of California, happiness is having the U.S. Supreme Court rule that Com-
munists do not have to register with the Government. "I
have been for a number of years, I am now, and I propose
to remain a member of the Communist Party of the
United States," she'd written. . . . Girlish glee goes with
grim ideology.

Women were still called "girls" and still adorned ads for cars,
alcohol, and cigarettes, though occasionally a female teacher could
be seen touting life insurance.

I Am Woman, Hear Me Roar

By the late 1960s and early 1970s, we had started wondering why
we had spent money, blood, sweat, and tears on an education if we
were still asked if we could type before applying for jobs. The want
ads were segregated into "male" and "female," even though it was
clear that in many cases, we could easily do the jobs advertised for
men only. This cognitive dissonance was then described by writer
Jane O'Reilly in Ms. magazine's preview issue as a "click," a kind of
late-twentieth-century "Eureka" phenomenon where women suddenly understood that the social forces keeping them in place where
our mothers had stood were now unacceptable. It could be simple
things, such as why women should have to do the dishes after family get-togethers while men settled in to watch the football or
hockey games. And it could be cosmic, as in why women could not
be priests—it was possible that the pope was wrong.

We started forming "consciousness-raising" groups, where we
were told never to refer to women as "girls" and where we collec-
tively began to understand that if we wanted more from life than
our mothers had enjoyed, then we would have to do something

about it. A few of us marched in demonstrations; some went back to business school or to law school or medical school. Many stayed in their jobs and determinedly pushed their way up the corporate ladder in an environment that slowly began to accept that women would be around the office for longer than the few years it used to take to "snag" a man. Thousands subscribed to the new voice of the women's movement, Ms. magazine, which took on a dizzying array of subjects in its first few years. It seemed that there was no subject Ms. could not give a feminist twist to: politics, housework, fixing a car, cosmetics, oppression of stewardesses and household workers, men's consciousness raising, prostitution, sex role stereotyping of children, the lack of women on the boards of major corporations, choosing not to have kids, "vaginal politics," who should cook dinner.

And then, and again very unlike our mothers' lives, we were given the power over our own reproductive systems. We could choose when (or if) we would have children. We could choose when (or if) to have sex. When the federal Food and Drug Administration approved the licensing of a 10-milligram pill, combining progestin and estrogen and labeled "The Pill," manufacturer G. D. Searle changed every woman's life forever. As Bernard Asbell says in The Pill, in 1965, the birthrate "dropped down to the national average from one that had been 50 percent higher. . . . Across the range of classes and pursuits, lives changed. The Pill enabled not only the planning of a family, but the planning of a life through the timing of a career."

Ladies' Home Journal celebrated the Pill's thirtieth birthday in 1990, telling readers that this small, white concoction of hormones

> transformed our lives like nothing before or since. . . . It's easy to forget how truly liberating The Pill seemed to be in 1960. Nothing else in this century—perhaps not even winning the right to vote—made such an immediate difference in women's lives. . . . It spurred sexual frankness and experimentation. It allowed

women to think seriously about careers because they could postpone childbirth. And it sparked the feminist and prochoice movement. Once women felt they were in charge of their own bodies, they began to question the authority of their husbands, their father, their bosses, their doctor, their church.

We were launched onto the merry-go-round of wanting more for ourselves in our professional lives, piloting a radical new course for ourselves than the one taken by mom, sometimes rejecting outright what she had advised us to do or not to do. Or, so we thought.

We rebelled and started on the long journey that would distinguish each of our lives: trying to understand our mothers and ourselves and the relationship we share.

Part II

The Fruits of Their Labor

3

Always Have
Something to Fall Back On

Mom said, "You are not going to be a secretary.
You are going to have one. Go to law school."
Francesca, thirty-six-year-old public defender, Chicago

It is striking how many women—even those who are Wandering Daughters—salute their mothers for having insisted they get a good education, which translated into getting a college degree or beyond. Despite our mothers' understandable inability to foresee the array of careers we would embark on, they knew this: we needed better education and preparation than they had. We definitely needed something to "fall back on," they warned us; we needed to hedge our bets. This advice turned out to serve us well as we weathered divorce and single parenthood, the need to be self-supporting because we never married, the need to participate fully in financially supporting our families, or simply the desire to travel the career paths available to us.

What propelled us to spend a lot of money and time on getting our degrees? For some of the early baby boomers, it was clearly a way to better ourselves or have a fuller, more secure life than did our mothers, who weren't necessarily happy playing Betty Crocker. Later, the women's movement gave us a theology for doing this, pointed out examples of successful women again and again, and made it seem natural that we do as our brothers did and get that degree.

Overwhelmingly our survey respondents rated their mothers' influence on education as positive. Sixty-three percent of those who said they didn't get along with their mothers as teenagers remember that even during those tangled years, their moms had a positive impact on their academic pursuits. Seventy percent of daughters who did get along with their moms during their teenage years also gave her full marks for affecting them positively when it came to education.

For baby boomer women, our mothers' advice on getting an education has turned out to be one of the single most important foundations for our lives. Their advice, "Get a good education so you'll have more than I did," has enabled us to travel far beyond the confines of their lives. As one respondent said, "Get an education was the most important advice she gave me. My mother never did, and she was, she felt, stuck in a marriage she sometimes desperately wanted to be out of, and I would never be stuck anywhere."

A nurse from Nebraska wrote: "She stressed that education and career were important. She had two daughters out of three who graduated from college. I think she wanted more for us than she got." And a computer programmer from Texas, now working on her master's degree, told us, "Both my parents were preaching education as early as I can remember, though the only careers for a woman were teaching, nursing, or being a mother."

Reflecting on their own lack of steady careers and an ensured source of income apart from their husband's, many respondents' mothers underscored the uncertainty that life held and the bulwark an education would erect. An educational administrator from Cincinnati says her mother repeated and repeated that she "'study hard, get good grades, get a college education,'" writes Susan. "She cautioned me that with an education, then 'You'll always be able to take care of yourself' afterward. This was her best advice because it's true."

Still, How Many
Words a Minute Can You Type?

Sometimes this mantra, "go to college, go to college," had an esteem and power that did not always guarantee we would be "living the Life of Riley." Respondents' mothers (particularly those on the front end of the baby boom) advised getting a teaching degree or a B.A. or majoring in the classics, not always instant tickets to well-paying or steady careers. On the other hand, the eclecticism and more generalized education we pursued ironically has made for stronger work skills since the modern workplace requires a flexibility that women may be better suited for than are men. We were reading Jane Austen and Nathaniel Hawthorne at college, but (for early baby boomers), we were also taking home economics. We were, as well, studying geography, math, biology, history, and, for some brave souls, even physics; but all the while, we were earning money baby-sitting and figuring out how to calm a crying child when we were only sixteen years old. In short, we were beginning the artful enterprise of juggling.

Many of us born in the 1940s and early 1950s believed a B.A. or teaching degree was all we would need, and our mothers promoted that kind of general education. Jennifer, a piano teacher in Riverview, Florida, remembers her mother's advice to major in the humanities. But, she recalls, "This wasn't so great because it led to nowhere in the job market. On the other hand, the subject matter interested me and, in the context of half a lifetime, has brought a lot of joy to me. I'm a lifelong student of the arts, an amateur nutritionist, psychologist, poet, you name it."

For Melinda, a magazine production manager in British Columbia, following in her mother's educational and work life footsteps seemed quite natural, even though she got a degree that was not an instant door opener. The value of a good liberal arts education—for both herself and her mother, who also worked in publishing—laid a solid intellectual foundation. "My mother," she said, "was the only woman to graduate from her college in philosophy in her year, and this impressed me a lot. I wanted to equal her intellectual prowess, so I pursued a fairly esoteric education, which I thoroughly enjoyed but which left me with few marketable skills. Nonetheless, I would repeat it and still appreciate the role model she was for a liberal arts education."

On the other side of the educational dividing line, there were daughters who did not have Melinda's "Philosopher Mom" to guide them and who saw their mother's lack of education as a stark reminder that they must do better. Carrie is a forty-six-year-old international business broker from Cincinnati with two master's degrees. Her mother had just two years of high school, so her career was limited to in-home demonstrations of Stanley Home Products and managing a retail store. If only her mother had the chance she had, writes Carrie:

> My mother was extremely smart and talented, but she married at sixteen and dropped out of school to escape an unhappy home life. She continued self-education, but never went back to school. On the other hand, I wanted to be formally educated because I knew she suffered in her self-esteem because of it. She thought I was smart, but not beautiful like her. So, education was my way out and up.

It is striking how well some daughters have done, all the while casting glances in their rearview mirrors at how severely limiting their moms' lack of education could be.

For many of the baby boomer women who did head off to college, there was also another piece of singular advice, which sometimes seemed contradictory: go to college, but learn to type. Learning to type would be an admission that we were headed for the secretarial pool, would it not? Our mothers, however, saw it as another hedge, and besides, it helped with term papers. Again, with great irony, now we look upon the skill as something almost essential in coping with the working world today. Fewer and fewer people (men and women) have secretaries to do the dictation, typing, and final product. These middle-level jobs are the ones that are quickly decreasing in the job market and listed as occupations whose future is limited. On the other hand, it's the people who can access PowerPoint, the Internet, and a word processing program who will advance or succeed in a career. Men too have had to learn to type (later in life than we did), but we were there first. Each sex was pigeonholed, especially at the beginning of the boom—boys were more likely urged to consider professional careers, while girls were advised to be secretaries, nurses, or teachers—because boys got better career counseling. After all, they would have to support a family, when all was said and done, right? Not necessarily, as it turns out. Given the number of baby boomer women who are supporting families, the humble skill of typing and then the more advanced skill of flexibility in adapting to new tasks has fitted us up for the modern world perhaps better than it did our brothers.

For Marianne, a human resources officer in Chicago, her mom's nagging about learning to type did turn out to be important. It came hand in hand with the admonition that she also go to college: "Mom's greatest advice was, 'go to college, and learn how to type.' Now I think I never could have realized this goal of education, never would have had it, if she didn't constantly encourage it. Learning to type actually has come in handy all my life. I took typing classes before high school, and it's helped me immensely in school and professional life."

How many of our brothers were being encouraged to take typing? Not many, to judge from our respondents. But that gave us a leg up on them.

Only in later years, particularly if they have children, have women in our survey understood that our mother's advice came at a cost: education was important but expensive. Lee, an educational administrator from Cincinnati, remembers this well. Her dad was a supply officer for a veterans' hospital, and, to save money for Lee's education, he and her mom decided to live on the army base, even though her mom wanted her own home. Her mother never moved into that home until she was sixty-six. Lee says that "it was planned from the time I started school that I attend college and as my mother saved for this expense, she often went without things for herself, like a new coat. Because of her and my father's encouragement, I almost always felt a sense of self and had a positive self-image. Not until I had children of my own did I realize how important an education is and how much was sacrificed by my family in order for me to be prepared to take care of myself."

The small minority of daughters in our survey whose mothers did not advise them that a good education was important still feel limited in their life choices. Several of these had mothers who had seriously advised their daughters that pursuing a college degree was the means to their "MRS.," which was, understandably, the kind of advice they had been given.

Federal Judge Susan Dlott

On December 29, 1995, Susan J. Dlott took her oath of office as a federal judge in the U.S. District Court for the Southern District of Ohio. A Democrat, she had been nominated by President Bill Clinton to this high office. Her nomination then had to be approved by the Republican-controlled Senate. Considering the acrimonious bashing of Clinton appointees to the bench that was taking place, this was yet another achievement. She was just forty-six at the time.

Susan Dlott's rise from Boston University School of Law to the first tier of courts in the United States was rapid. She clerked for the Ohio Court of Appeals, became an assistant U.S. attorney, and then worked for a prestigious law firm in Cincinnati where she became a partner, a notable achievement in a conservative city with just two other women partners in city law firms. She was tenacious in the courtroom, well prepared, tough, and fair.

At first blush, it might appear that because Judge Dlott's mother, Mildred Zemboch Dlott, was "just a housewife," her father must have been the driving force behind her remarkable academic and career achievements. But that assumption would be wrong. Only now, when Susan sits back and sifts the evidence, does she explain that her mother deserves much credit for what she has achieved.

At age nineteen, after one year of college, Mildred married her high school sweetheart, Herman Dlott, who owned a heavy precision machine tool shop that grew from a handful of employees to a successful business of one hundred employees. Susan describes her mother as very bright, but afraid to leave Dayton, Ohio, for long. Mrs. Dlott took up stamp collecting with some enthusiasm, did volunteer work, and raised three children, reminding them all the time that they would be expected to do well in school and attend a good college. Susan's father would have been happy for his children to go to Ohio State University, but that was not good enough for Mrs. Dlott, who encouraged Ivy League schools for her three children. For Susan, it was the University of Pennsylvania as an undergraduate and then onto Boston Law School, an excellent foundation for her career as a lawyer and judge. Says Dlott:

> My mother's greatest influence on me was achieving at school, although my father was the stimulus for that too, but in a negative way. With my father, nothing we ever did, or at least my perception is that nothing I ever did, was good enough, whatever I did! It could be all A's, and he would say, "Couldn't you do better?" And I would always feel like a failure in his eyes. But in my mother's eyes, at least I always felt successful in school. She also always said to me, "You're a late bloomer." It probably had a negative influence on me in my teens and even into my twenties, thinking, "That's why I'm not popular," "I shouldn't even strive to be because I'm not interesting; I don't have anything to offer that anybody my age would be interested in." But I think it's kind of funny

that I am, finally, a late bloomer. You know, I finally seem to be hitting my stride in my mid-forties. By the time I'm sixty, I should peak, which is better than the people who peaked in high school!

Susan Dlott is grateful to her mother for insisting she travel to the East and finish her education, even though she herself had vacated that career track. Like many other women in this survey, she believes she is having the career that her mother could have had at another time and in another place. And although she idolized her father for the power she thought he had when she was growing up, now Susan looks to her mother as the stronger of the two:

I think about her all the time, especially now, professionally. I think that I want to be what she could have been. I want to be the professional that she had the ability to be and just didn't have the education and time to be because she devoted it to us as children instead of putting it into a career. I don't think of my father now as my role model; I think of my mother. And that's a huge shift. I wanted to be in business in my twenties, and even in my thirties, I wanted to be the professional that I thought my father was. But now I want to be the professional my mother could have been. She had unlimited potential because she has a greater intellect than he does, and she's tougher than he is. She has this steadfastness, this core, this moral compass that wasn't as strong in him. You know that when she set her mind to something, nothing would deter her.

Susan Dlott is no longer the klutz or the late bloomer, in her mother's eyes. Her unqualified love and pride in her daughter mean that "if I were on death row, she would still think I was the most wonderful kid in the world," says Susan.

Baby Boomer Women's Careers:
A Kaleidoscope of Choices

Armed with better-than-ever educations, baby boomer women have achieved an independence their mothers sometimes thought they saw down the road; at other times, it was an outgrowth. Some, like Mary Rita, an office manager from Chicago, believe that above all other advice, the most important value her mother passed on to her was "independence and self-preservation." As the single mother of a twenty-year-old daughter, she wants to know that her "daughter can also stand on her own two feet, that when the chips are down, she'll know how to pick them up; have the ability, the ingenuity when ability falters, and the strength of character to do what's necessary to survive without walking over or using people."

Respondents note that often their mothers were not independent of their husband's control, but they wished for that degree of freedom for their daughters, even if they could not have it for themselves. Often fathers too encouraged their daughters to find their own way. Our mothers' world had changed greatly through the Depression, World War II, and then the 1950s, a time when conformity could be rigidly enforced. Now mothers encouraged their daughters to "look out for yourself," as one put it, or, "Nobody will take as good care of you as you do for yourself." As Ann, a substitute teacher from Illinois, put it, "My mother's best advice was to finish my education and then be self-reliant and don't depend on anyone except myself."

The careers undertaken by our respondents are wide-ranging and eclectic; their achievements present a kaleidoscope of patterns. These daughters have roamed further and wider than their mothers did, and their contribution to society through their careers has been substantial. There are homemakers in the survey, though many of them value the education they got as a way to enhance their own children's educations and their ability to be wise mothers and wives. For many, homemaking is a temporary "career" in between those they had before marriage and those they intend to resume. Some respondents are nurses, teachers, social workers, and secretaries, which are the same occupations that were deemed permissible for their mothers. But within those fields, daughters have gone beyond tradition and now list the following occupations too: doctor, psychologist, physical fitness consultant, paramedic, physician assistant, emergency room registrar, public health administrator, medical transcription services owner, optometrist, special education consultant, university professor, educational administrator, and office manager. In the health care industry, the rise of the nurse-administrator is remarkable. In the 1950s, the nurse was the handmaiden of the doctor. Now someone with an R.N. degree has the same chance as a physician to be in charge of committees in the billion-dollar, managed health care industry. That industry's ranks are overrepresented by women, and increasingly those women are in managerial roles.

For our respondents, add to our pot of stew the following: journalist, publisher, writer, lawyer, playwright, screenwriter, musicians, actress, aerobics dance champion, songwriter, choreographer, flight attendant, engineer, management trainer, account executive, comptroller, financial analyst, computer programmer, human resources manager, corporate trainer, consumer research manager, international broker, events planner. In the mix we have intuitive arts counselors, dog sitters, and one owner of a horse farm. Where before our mothers demonstrated Avon products, we are selling fine wines. Where our mothers were cooks, we now are chefs and consultants to the food industry. The choices we made were not always wise or what best suited us, but the greatest majority credit their mothers with positively influencing the career paths they ultimately took.

Like our mothers, many of our career paths zigzag from one place to the next. Unlike our mothers, these changes take place generally in the professional world. There is a determination not to be just like mom, but to take her advice and learn from her (and from her mistakes). As Diana, an insurance agent in Indiana, put it, "I knew I didn't want to be a sales clerk all my life, like her." Or, like Judge

Dlott, respondents were motivated by their mothers' *lack* of a career. Jean, a physician from Cincinnati, remembers "growing up and thinking this woman [her mother] should be working, this woman should have a career. She is not happy doing what she's doing."

Mother to Daughter:
Don't Do As I Did, Do As I Say

Our respondents took their mother's advice about perseverance and pioneering and followed careers they admit their mothers did not necessarily envision but nevertheless usually applaud. Mothers were held back by social expectations that they really belonged in the home and nowhere else, and they usually internalized these expectations. The daughters in our survey report that their mothers pushed them either overtly or covertly into another world, that of careers and work. Lillian is a singer-songwriter who is pursuing this unorthodox and uncertain career with her mother's full support. She reports that her eighty-one-year-old mother also tried being a professional singer herself but quit to have children. She writes: "Although my mom's self-esteem has always been low, she's always said things to me like, 'You're so talented—you're more talented than I ever was.' She has financially supported my music career and encouraged me to pursue it, telling me she has no doubt I have the talent and ability. She said my dad prevented her from a career and that I shouldn't let anyone do that to me."

Some daughters have eventually wound up in careers their mothers did encourage, but at the time when they were making career choices, they were also rebelling against their mothers. It was hard to see that mothers could have assessed our talents and matched them with job opportunities, but sometimes they were correct. This is so with daughters who chose more traditional careers, such as Sandra, a special education teacher, who rejected her mother's advice about a lot of things, and when that advice was being handed out, she felt her mother was "intruding." She recalls that "even though mom was right, it would have caused fewer hard feelings and arguments had she let me figure things out on my own, as I eventually did anyway. Since I was small, she told me I should be a teacher. Then she continued telling me that throughout my young adulthood—despite the fact that I was very successful in the real estate business. Every time I was unhappy with a job or a client, she'd encourage me to go back to school and become a teacher. So, I did. And I love it!!"

Nonetheless, some respondents think the traditional career track they took, at their mother's behest, has been a route that has been too conventional and risk free, albeit better than not having finished college and had any sort of career at all. Beth, a human resources manager who's worked in the banking and nonprofit sectors, thanks her mother (who worked as a maid and then in a factory) for urging her to do her homework, get good grades, and pursue a degree. "If I hadn't," she said, "I'd probably be like most of the women in my high school class who didn't pursue degrees and who have stayed in town in secretarial jobs." On the other hand, her mother's worst advice was to comply with conventional behaviors and not to draw attention to oneself. Writes Beth, "It's the worst advice because in many ways, it has kept me from taking risks in my career and encouraged conformity and kept me from expressing the uniqueness of me."

Some respondents now recognize that they have fashioned careers out of skills they learned at their mother's knee, and they are surprised but pleased. Cora, for example, has turned the purchase of a video camera in 1980 into a business where she develops and markets videos for sale. In her past, she has sold crafts and done woodwork and is proud of her entrepreneurial spirit. Where did she get that from? Her mom, she argues. It may be that her mother knew nothing about videos, but her mother's "pioneer spirit, the confidence and the courage to do things whether or not you know how," are the gifts her mother has given her. It was not until she was in her forties that Cora figured this out: "I was in a seminar on money and was asked to write my own and my family's money history. I started laughing because I was *nothing* like my dad's family, but just like my mom's, which was full of hustlers. Like her dad, I looked for a need and figured out how to fill it and make a few bucks at the same time. Now I can see Mom's good points, her pioneer spirit that sees breakdowns as temporary setbacks and just figures out how to keep going."

For African American women in our survey, the chances of success (theirs and their mothers') were fewer than those available to white women, so their career achievements are even more remarkable. Lisa is the executive director of a housing agency in Cincinnati and credits her unblinking pursuit of a career to her mother's influence:

> I had always thought that black women were professionals, period. I mean, it was kind of like, "Your mother doesn't work?!" My mother was a sickle cell counselor for a veterans' hospital, and my grandmother was selling real estate in the 1950s. I always thought everybody goes to college. Everybody is supposed to have a career, and the five years that I stayed home with my two children made me insane. I just had this burning career desire, and I had to go out and I had to do things, and I had to finish up this other degree [an M.B.A.]. My mother did stay home with us, but my memory bank says that I always saw her going to work and I always saw my grandmother as a professional and that's what I wanted to do.

Jeannelle, an African American engineer from Chicago, also had a working mother who had attended college and told her daughter she would too. "Good grades are their own reward," she remembers her mother telling her. Now an airline engineer, Jeannelle thanks her mother for making her independent and forcing her to do things for herself, though she resented this as a teenager.

Now, says Jeannelle, it has everything to do with her successful career, which has provided her with financial security. Should she have to, she would be able to support her two children on her own.

Maureen Kempston Darkes, Vice President of General Motors

In all the press reports during the General Motors of Canada strike of 26 thousand workers for twenty-one days in the autumn of 1996, little mention seemed to be made in the American media that the president of this giant corporation (and vice president of General Motors Corporate) was a woman. Since Catalyst, a woman's group, estimates that only 10 percent of corporate officers at North America's Fortune 500 companies are women, it was certainly an oversight, though perhaps a sign that women have started to arrive and that their presence is no longer remarkable. The impact of the GM Canada strike at U.S. plants idled another 18 thousand U.S. workers.

Maureen Kempston Darkes is a woman of competence, determination, and calm, who runs what is Canada's largest manufacturer, providing one in six jobs in Ontario and earning a record profit of $98 million in 1995. The strike was over the difficult issue of outsourcing component parts for GM vehicles from non-GM suppliers, something businesses do (with varying frequencies) to stay competitive in the North American auto market.

Hers was not a childhood of privilege, of a father's urging his daughter to go into a man's world and providing the financial resources to do it. Instead, Maureen Kempston Darkes's Irish mother made that happen. She raised Maureen and her two brothers on her own, earning her living as a secretary in a bank after the death of her husband, keeping house and making sure her children were well educated. For Maureen, that led to an undergraduate degree in history and political science and then law school at one of Canada's best universities, the University of Toronto. For her brothers, it was medicine and dentistry. Again, as with most other women on the front end of the baby boom, law school (not to mention General Motors) was not exactly what Mrs. Kempston envisioned, but her vigorous, determined, and focused voice urged Maureen to persevere, even when it annoyed her daughter and even when she wanted to "goof off" with her friends during adolescence.

How did Kempston Darkes reach the top? She gives credit to her mother's tenacity and determination, in the face of little financial or societal support. Like most other baby boomer women, she rebelled (though only slightly) at her mother's view of what she needed to do:

> When you are in our situation, you really have to support each other, and I think as kids we recognized how hard it was for Mum. I was taught that we had to support one another. For us, education was the way to a better life. We couldn't generate a whole lot of income, but we wanted to get ahead in society. My mother would say, "You'll go through some hard times, but you have some tremendous opportunities ahead of you." But you can imagine as teenagers, you get a little tired of hearing that! You want to goof off—you hear what all these other teenagers are doing and whatever—but that wasn't an option for us. So, we were very much focused.

Widows in the 1950s and 1960s were generally left out of social occasions, and Maureen believes that her mother's life was lonely because of this convention. Still, through it all, her mother fostered her children's beliefs in their abilities with advice similar to that voiced by Ulysses in Tennyson's poem, where the old sailor urged his crew "to strive, to seek, to find and not to yield":

> What has always stuck with me is the sad side and the happy side of her life. The sad side is that I saw a woman who was dealt a pretty tough hand—losing my dad,

going to work—but who basically said throughout her life, "There don't have to be barriers. Do what you want. You can achieve what you want to achieve; you just need to set your sights high, you need to make a commitment to get there, and you need a set of core values in your life. If you do that, you will have a good life. And always remember, stick to your core values, to those values that made you happy." That was the happy side of it.

The hard side was to understand what a woman goes through when she loses a spouse. In my mother's day, they were expected to get married for life. They didn't have all the educational opportunities that we had. And I always felt very badly that my Mum didn't have the support. It bothered me as a kid that she didn't have a lot of things that I saw other kids' mothers had. I found that my mother's life was hard. At the same time, I learned by watching Mum that you have to make your own way in this world, that you have to be prepared for what God deals, and you have to be prepared to contribute and to continue on with your life, to find happiness, just do what's right and what is expected of you. Her life, I thought, was just more difficult. That was how society was: you did things in couples. I think things are different nowadays. I think society has progressed; it's a much more open society today. My mother never described herself as a feminist, but in many ways she felt you have to make your life, to achieve.

General Motors was not something Maureen's mother would have foreseen, nor was law school, but, as Maureen said, "there was one thing I learned, and that was you grow to opportunities. But if you've got a sense of adventure, then opportunities will come. You just have to take hold of the right one. That was also her philosophy. She would say, 'When opportunity comes, reach out.' It was the same with General Motors: when opportunity came, I just reached out."

We Now Can Manage Our Own Finances

The funny thing was that even though mothers were often not earning a paycheck, they frequently controlled how it was spent. Judge Dlott remembers that her mother and father had separate domains—he ran his business, and she ran the house. "She decided if we were going to buy a new house, if she was going to buy furniture, if she was going to send us to camp. Anything that related to the house and the children was totally her decision, and anything outside—if he bought a new business, a new machine, a new car, or whatever else—was his domain. They were executives of their own domain."

Rachelle, a closing officer for a builder in Chicago, writes that her mother held the purse strings in her family, even though her mom took time off from working to raise four children until her last, Rachelle, was in junior high. As Rachelle remembers, "My father wouldn't know how to write a check if his life depended on it. Mom always handled all those kind of things and still does. She always knows exactly where the money is going and things like that." Rachelle, who is married to a salesman, also handles her family's finances and is surprised when she finds other women do not: "I've run into friends whose husbands control all the money and give them basically spending money, and I find that peculiar because I'm the one that handles all the finances. I suppose it's because my mother always did."

And so, hand in hand with education, leading to independence and a career, baby boomer women thank their moms for having made them aware of how important it is to understand finances. Sometimes it was the homey "Be thrifty" or "Save for a rainy day," or "Use it up, wear it out, make it do, or do without." Often it was a conservative view of investing, summed up in one mother's often-repeated clichés her daughter remembers: "Always put a little from each paycheck into the bank" and "Save the pennies, and the pounds will take care of themselves." On occasion, the advice was even more pointed. If mothers did not handle the finances—or even if they did—they counseled their daughters to do so. Says Marjorie, a property manager in Cincinnati who is married, with one son: "My mother's greatest advice was 'Manage the money in your house-hold, and don't let a man control your life like I did.' It was great advice because my father controlled their money, and I didn't approve of that. Mother never saw his paychecks. That would not happen in my life."

As baby boomer women face widowhood, that advice about being very involved in the family finances will prove important, par-ticularly given the unsettling predictions about what will happen to Social Security when we begin to turn sixty-five. Analysts bemoan this generation's lack of savings, but some baby boomer women know what they should do, because their mothers told them so. Marie, a nurse from Chicago, has three children and was re-cently widowed. Her mother's greatest advice to her was: "'Always have a secret stash of money that your husband doesn't know about.' It's great advice because I'm able to support myself and my children since I was widowed unexpectedly. I had money to fall back on." Other mothers have suggested that it is possible for their daughters to be prepared to support themselves, but to do it openly. Deirdre, the medical transcriptionist from Chicago, now believes her mother was right about this. "She always told me to maintain my own money and not to rely totally on another person for my well-being, to be my own person, to be responsible. She didn't mean to be sneaky or devious—just to maintain my independence."

Stand On Your Own Two Feet

*I now realize how strong she was after our family
losses, and I'm aware of how she sheltered me during
family crises but still made me aware of the world.
She helped me be the strong, dependable person I am.*
Julianna, forty-five-year-old physician, Dallas

If our mothers suspected we would have an easier time of things than they had, they nevertheless instilled in us the need for strength and backbone to overcome whatever struggles we would face. Sometimes our lives have been harder than our mothers' (though the majority of respondents think their lives are simply different); sometimes they have been easier. Whatever we have come up against and however we have triumphed or just managed to survive, the wisdom of our mothers has been there for us, like a small seed that grows with time or an unused muscle that we can suddenly flex.

An amazing litany of truisms has floated down from our mothers. Sometimes it came with a strong masculine dose: "You can be whatever you want to be; nothing will stand in your way." Sometimes it was a more feminine, accommodating style of accepting people for what they are and making do, or as one mother told her daughter, time after time, "Life is just what you make of it." We have mixed and matched these, some respondents favoring one style over the other, but it seems to have worked.

Our mothers weathered an enormous amount of change in their lives, all the while being expected to carry on and produce a family and home that rigorously adhered to the rigid mores of the 1950s and early to mid-1960s. They had few support systems—unlike their daughters—and were, with some exceptions, surrounded by little trustworthy advice that could be easily accessed. From doctors' advocating smoking, to women's magazines touting the importance of staying at home whatever the cost and partaking of the growing consumer culture, moms had to turn inward for strength. They coped when things went wrong, had to find a way around the problems, and had to be tough and resilient. And, no surprise, according to the daughters in our survey, these mothers bequeathed to their daughters those same characteristics. Sophie, a professional fundraiser, says, "My mother's greatest impact was in strength of character, for me to be strong and to stand up for myself and my beliefs; to be able to live through anything, no matter how difficult."

Sophie's view is echoed by many of the women in our survey. In fact, their responses about character and tenacity echo what the long-winded Polonius in Hamlet tells his son, Laertes. As Laertes is about to set out on an important journey, his father tells him: "To thine own self be true/And it must follow, as the night the day/Thou canst not then be false to any man." (Poor Ophelia is stuck back at the castle. Her "job," according to her brother, Laertes, is to keep clear of Hamlet, who has been acting very strangely, and to guard her virtue.) Maureen, a former legislative aide to an Illinois state senator, remembers her mother's advice was like that of Polonius's: "to believe in myself, which gives me a sense of self-worth and the strength not to rely on others' opinions. Plus, it's given me inner strength." Gillian, a school administrator, puts it this way: "My mother's greatest influence is on my sense of self. She's not had an easy life, yet she maintains (or really has developed) a strong set of personal attributes. She doesn't expect others to live by her rules, only herself. She's taught me to be true to myself and to develop that self. Life's not easy, and she doesn't try to pretend it is or to change it—just how to go with it and be happy."

Divorce and Other Hardships: A Silver Lining

For many respondents whose mothers were divorced, their mother's example—of a woman forced to cope and stay strong for her children—was vivid and affirming. Cheryl Marie, a teacher and consultant from Illinois, says, "My mother was very tempted, when my father left her, to give my brother and me to an aunt and uncle to raise, feeling that she couldn't possibly go on alone. She did go on, and things were tough sometimes. But we all managed to stay together."

Ellie, the culinary consultant from Chicago, thinks about her mother like clockwork, and her thoughts are often about how difficult it was for her mother to raise her alone, as a woman born in Russia, living among her Russian relatives in suburban Detroit—but divorced:

> I admire my mother's determination for achieving her goals. She was a woman of the nineties but living in the fifties and sixties. When she was divorced with a child in 1958, that was frowned upon. At the veterans' hospital where she worked, they dealt with drug addiction, and they were starting to get Vietnam vets there, so it was not an easy time, and she dealt with most of this.
>
> When my mother came to the United States, she was the only child. But then, my grandmother had five boys right in a row, and she was the babysitter, helping my grandmother with the family, going to summer school for English. I didn't have that; I was an only child. The

other thing is, my grandfather was an alcoholic, and his brother's wife was a bootlegger. My grandfather worked on the line at Ford in Dearborn [Michigan]. My grandmother would go to the gate when he got paid and get his paycheck and take the pay away from him. Then, there was the Depression and everything that came along with that.

The terrible toll that divorce took on our mothers and their families and the limited options available to women of that generation have made these maternal survival skills critical resources for their daughters as well. Frances, a thirty-seven-year-old financial analyst in California, remembers that when her father left her mother, the two daughters were ultimately left with a large gift: their mother's strength:

When my dad left Mom and us when I was sixteen years old, she sort of fell apart for awhile. The parenting level went away in some aspects. But through the worst part of the split-up, Mom was still able to get a job as a teaching assistant, as well as studying, at the junior college, and she was on the honor roll. She always made sure we knew that the three of us were important. She also made sure we knew that other people around us felt we were important. I have never doubted that I was an important person and that I was important to be on this earth.

Frances's mom raised her two daughters working in property management after college and her divorce. (Before that, she'd been a church school director and the owner of a plant store.)

Life Is Just What You Make of It

Of course, even mothers who were not divorced had to cope with more than their share of burdens from time to time. An accountant from Colorado relates how her mother, married for thirty-five years, "raised nine children and was, for many years, the main family breadwinner. She has suffered through many losses of people she loved and still remained the strongest person I have ever known. She has always had a very strong faith in God and says that's what gets her through. I didn't realize how strong, hard working, and giving she was." Colleen, now the mother of four children and divorced, remembers how her mother, while busy earning the family's income, let her kids know "she loved us and we could go to her for help, and she would tell me, 'You have very strong willpower. You can do it.'"

Daughters—whether married, divorced, widowed, or unhappily married—report learning from their mothers that they would have to "stand on their own two feet" if they were to survive. Greta is one who saw her mother working from the time she was eighteen, all through her marriage, five children, and widowhood at age fifty-five. Her mother's jobs were menial—dry cleaning helper, nursing home, factory work—until she took over management of the K-Mart snack bar for twenty years. Her father also worked in the dry cleaner and then took on the job of a crane operator for twenty-five years, until his retirement. Through it all, Greta says, "I learned that a woman must depend on herself and her own strength and that the burden of responsibility most often falls to her alone. Intellectually, I may know this may not always be the case—but at a gut level, I see it true more often than not."

Much of this recognition of our mother's strength and resilience takes place after the daughters have grown. In response to our question, "If your view of your mother has changed since you were a teenager, describe what is different," Margot, a forty-six-year-old teacher's aide and homemaker, writes: "I recognize the struggling, hard work and pain, and stick-to-itness she endured and admire her the more for it." Margot's mother raised four girls and a boy and worked most of the time they were growing up at low-paying jobs— at a dry cleaner, then at a senior citizens' home at night, and then at a cheese factory:

> I understand now some of the how and whys of the way things were back then. Mom married young, had kids young, worked constantly inside and outside the home. We were provided for but were never looked upon as individuals to become friends with. Regretfully we remember a lot of the hard times: Dad drinking, the fighting, the tears, the must-be-quiet times afterward, the guilt feelings for taking sides. My "formative years," until I was almost five, were spent with my maternal grandmother, and my very first memories are of her. I still don't know my mom's "innards." She's happy, and we are friends. I know what not to do with my own kids. I love her dearly but with a sad regret sometimes.

Another respondent, Doreen, a fifty-year-old mother with two kids, who works as a market research consultant, says that her view of her mother has totally changed:

> I was very smart and very ready to correct her grammar or pronunciation or whatever else she might do wrong. I always beat her at games. And, I realize that giving me the example of a woman's making decisions and running machines was invaluable. I never got the impression that the world stopped at our picket fence or that you can't fight city hall. In other words, I was not disempowered.

I felt like I kind of raised myself, since I was such a loner,
but still the example I had of a woman was of a powerful one.

It's not necessary that women see their mothers as saints in order
to reach this conclusion. Yet respondents' recognition of their
mothers' merits is at the heart of the mother-daughter journey. Even
Renee, the physician who is very critical of her mother, knows the
power of a mother's strength and that its passage from one generation to another puts women ahead of men:

I think it is just that daughters sense the strength that
mothers have, no matter what they have done, whereas
I'm not sure that husbands or sons know that strength
that mothers have, much like daughters do. I don't know
that my brother understands the surviving nature of my
mother at this point in her life, like my sister and I sort
of sense about her.

The things we fought about with our mothers—from the sub-
lime to the ridiculous (our right to choose our friends, say, versus
getting our ears pierced)—begin to take on a new slant as we gain
maturity. Some respondents complain that it was a pity that time
was wasted on the mundane, but they respect the tension and
arguments over larger issues that now shape their lives in ways that
surprise them.

Sophie, the professional fundraiser in Ohio, reports that when
she was a high school freshman, her mother discovered that
Sophie's back was crooked. She marched her off to the best ortho-
pedists, who diagnosed Sophie with scoliosis. Eighty percent of people diagnosed with curvature of the spine are children, and doctors
recommend early, prompt intervention, usually by fitting the patient

with a brace to prevent a significant deformity. Sophie's father was the associate chairman of psychiatry at Michigan State University Medical School while her mother was a full-time homemaker for her husband, Sophie, and her sister. But it was Sophie's mother who took her medical crisis in hand, dealing with the doctors, the hospitals, and the complications. It was she who took Sophie for monthly visits from their home in East Lansing to clinics in Minneapolis and Milwaukee.

Sophie has grown to be tall, healthy, athletic, and attractive. During her first marriage, she taught aerobics, "which in Cleveland, was considered as glamorous as being a movie star," she says. Sophie remembers her mother's strength:

> She was a tough, outspoken, convincing woman who rarely (if ever) doubted her decisions, whose greatest legacy to her daughters was strength of character: to be strong and to stand up for myself and my beliefs, to be able to live through anything, no matter how difficult. I respect her for her ideas, her strength, and her ability to take care of other people. I also see that her views were shaped during a different time and that they don't necessarily hold true for me. I have my empathy for what she went through when I was a teenager and know that she wasn't being mean to me, making me wear a back brace. Rather, she was scared for my health.

Do we have what it takes—what she had or still has? we often wonder to ourselves. Jennifer, the saleswoman from Illinois, is asking herself that question about her mother, whose advice she once discounted: "My mom said, 'Live every day with joy!' She has survived breast cancer and colon cancer. The day after surgery, she was sitting up doing her nails! I admire that kind of strength. I hope I have it."

We Get It (Better Late Than Never)

Sometimes a mother's strength can be potent and overwhelming. It takes time on our journey to stand back from this force, assess its merits, and then fashion this gift of strength to suit our own lives. Janice, the international banking financier whose mother moved from volunteering to acting as village president and treasurer of the Garden Club of America, seemed overpowering to her daughter: "As a teenager, I felt very powerless in the face of a very strong-willed, able, and domineering woman. As an adult, I've managed to shift the power balance so that we lead our separate lives, and conflict is minimized."

We can come to recognize her strength in us after our own divorce or other traumatic events that seem to put us off course. Mae, like many of us, had to hit that wall before she turned to see her mother's figure beckoning her to carry on. She has taught in public and private schools in seven states and now lists herself as a school administrator. Although she believes that despite her teenaged "know-it-all, snotty attitude," she generally got along with her mother and found her mother and her mother's wisdom after a failed first marriage: "While I was very aware early on that we shared some likes/dislikes and values, I think I purposely fought to see any similarities during my high school and college years. After a disastrous first marriage (or perhaps during this time when I was twenty-eight), I began to be more comfortable with myself and was able to really connect with my mom once again. At this point, I was feeling very vulnerable, yet found great inner strength—one of my mother's strongest traits."

Strength to strength, from mother to daughter, is a common theme in the stories and questionnaires we received from our respondents. They see this with little doubt and as quite a marvelous gift now that they look back. Sometimes an outsider might not know we possess this strength and courage, but we know it is there when we need it. For women of accomplishment, including two who we met on our travels, it is the key to their own success.

Sandra Rivers, Pianist

When Sandra Rivers lays her hands on the keyboard of the grand piano in a concert hall, the piano, and thus the audience, are in her control. One of the world's top five accompanists at age forty-nine, she is beginning her career as a solo artist. Before, she was the person who would accompany violinist Nadja Salerno-Sonnenberg or soprano Kathleen Battle. Now she plays by herself and solos with the Dallas Symphony, the Louisiana Philharmonic, and the Cincinnati Symphony. Her mother would no doubt approve of this move. Her strength and certainty of purpose eventually reached her daughter's heart and continue to propel Sandra further into the tough world of classical music.

The route to Sandra Rivers's studio at the University of Cincinnati's College-Conservatory of Music is a maze of corridors and solitary, broken chairs leaning against dull-colored walls. But seeping through this forbidding landscape are the joyful sounds of music students' singing and playing their instruments. We eventually arrive at a door that looks like all the other doors lining the halls, and knock; as she opens the door, Rivers's wide grin and bright eyes greet us, melting away the late spring frost we have found in the halls. Her bare studio is filled with two Steinways (which have obviously put in a number of years on the job) and posters advertising her performances in New York and Spain with violinist Cho-liang Lin and soprano Kathleen Battle. Rivers is delighted to talk about her mother and the slow but steady route she has taken in her musical career.

In the early 1940s, Harlem, or "Sugar Hill," was an exciting place to live. Pauline and Bryan Rivers moved there from South Carolina to escape their large, meddling families ("they stayed in

everybody's business," says Sandra). Pauline was a singer and studied for a time at the Institute of Musical Art (the predecessor of
Julliard School of Music in New York City). She also worked on
and off Broadway in the chorus and toured with an African American chorus group. Bryan was both a pianist and organist, and
together their marriage was one of mutual harmony. Pauline had
several stillbirths, so by the time she gave birth to Sandra in 1947
when she was forty, Pauline decided to stay home and raise her
child. Pauline and Bryan carried on with their music, she teaching
voice and he the organ. Sandra says she can remember the musical sounds of these lessons floating over her crib. When she was
four, her father thought the time ripe to begin teaching his tiny
daughter how to play the piano.

As Sandra made her way through school, both regular and for
the gifted, she acquired her best, strongest, and most persistent
"agent" in the form of her mother. By the time she was in junior
high and needed financial assistance to get into Julliard Prep and
then the Professional Children's School, money was an issue. It was
up to Sandra to get the grades and pass the auditions; it was up to
Pauline to talk the school into admitting her daughter for a very
low fee or a scholarship. At age eleven, Sandra auditioned for and
was accepted at Julliard Preparatory School, the place where Pauline
began to hone her role as her daughter's agent, afraid of no one and
nothing. This woman without a big bank account from Harlem was
a force to be reckoned with: "My mother would say to the director
[of Julliard Prep], 'Maybe you have never given this amount [of
money] before, but you are going to accept her—we have no
money.' Now, a lot of parents don't do that. They are not going to
go up to a director who is forbidding and aloof and everybody else
is running the other way."

At Julliard, Sandra learned how to play for the best under
tremendous pressure; by the time she was ready for high school,
Pauline thought the best place for Sandra would be New York's

High School of Music and Art, a private school. But again, the Rivers bank account could not possibly pay for this.

Sitting back on one of the chairs lining the walls of her studio, Rivers remembers her mother's chutzpah:

> My mother asked if I was interested in pursuing this, and of course I said yes. I wanted to go to private school. I wanted to see what would happen. And so she went in and spoke to the director and told her about our financial situation. And I went in and took the tests and all this stuff, and they accepted me. And then my mother had that long talk with me about how my life would change if I went to Music and Art. It was integrated, and I would be the only black in my grade. So when it would be time to go home, I'd go my way and everyone else went theirs. She was letting me know what my social life would be like: Did I want to make these sacrifices to be able to say I went to private school? So it was laid out before me, and I chose it. If there was something to be hammered out, Mom had to take care of it. My mother didn't walk around being the perfect lady. You know—she spoke up. So when things needed to get done, they got done because my mother was there.

Pauline Rivers died when Sandra was twenty-nine, creating a deep hole in Sandra's heart. Sandra had not socialized extensively; her mother was very much the largest part of her life. But the strength of her mother seemed to have passed into her hands, and she found she had learned well when she had to deal with Pauline's sister over her mother's funeral arrangements:

> I came into my own when my mother passed. Her sister—who was also a force—came to help me with the

funeral arrangements, and I had never talked back to anyone or anything like that. But I started putting in my two cents, and all of a sudden, I just thought that maybe some of all this stuff has rubbed off on me and that I was quiet all these years. Now I am coming into my own, being my mother's daughter. People were shocked when I would speak up for stuff and not let anyone walk over me. Even my aunt was taken aback because I had never spoken back to her before. But I just stood on my own two feet. I said to myself, "You are a grown woman, you are not a child, and if you want something, this is the way it has to be. This is MY mother's funeral, it's not your mother's funeral, and this is what I want!"

Today Rivers still thinks she prefers to be nonconfrontational, but if she has to wrestle a problem to the ground, Pauline's daughter is ready for the challenge:

When I think about my mother, I realize how much education she had and all the advantages I had that she didn't have and what she was able to do as a woman back then. I think that's what influenced me, because she instilled in me so strongly to be a good person. She would say, "If you are given a talent, do the best you can with it, but you are not better than anybody else. Cause there is somebody out there that can do better than you." And just watching her live life and doing right by everybody else, people respecting her. She didn't have a doctorate, and she didn't go to college. And I keep thinking, "What if she had the advantages I had? There would have been no stopping her."

Sandra Rivers now teaches gifted piano students at the University of Cincinnati, enabling them to reach their potential and encouraging them to climb to the top of their profession—or at least to be the very best pianists their ability will allow.

———————

Several months after meeting Sandra, we drove to London, Ontario, to interview another artist who was also teaching young students, this time dancers, assisting them in choreographing a piece for a later performance. She, too, found her mother's strength to be a building block for her career in the arts.

Margie Gillis, Choreographer and Dancer

Like the mothers of so many other women in our survey, Margie Gillis's mother meant to live a life roughly resembling *Life* magazine ads, except that Margie's mum was an extraordinary athlete and an extraordinary person. So is her daughter.

When Margie Gillis appears on stage—and she is almost always alone—she pulls each member of the audience into her special arc. Canada's "Isadora Duncan," she is a solo dance artist from Montreal and was the first to introduce modern dance to China in 1979, after the Cultural Revolution. Hers is an unusual combination of athleticism, poetry, and insight as she dances in bare feet to music that can range from the Talking Heads to Sinead O'Connor to opera diva Jessye Norman. On the dance floor as in her life, Margie takes chances in the more than fifty works she has choreographed. Former Canadian prime minister Pierre Trudeau named her a Canadian Cultural Ambassador in 1981, and in 1988 she was appointed to the Order of Canada by the governor general, the highest award an artist can achieve in Canada. She has performed around the world, including frequently in the United States.

When we caught up with Margie, she was choreographing a piece with dance students in London, Ontario. It is no surprise that Margie's mother is also unforgettable, unique, and strong.

Rhona Wurtele, Margie's mother, and Rhona's twin sister, Rhoda, represented Canada's downhill ski team at the 1948 St. Moritz Olympics, which is where they met Margie's father, a hand-some and charismatic fellow who skied for the U.S. downhill team. The twins were named Canada's top athletes in 1944 for their skiing and swimming (they lost out the next year to a football player), and for the next few years, they dominated the field in skiing. They won the U.S. Nationals in 1946 and took the Kate Smith Trophy at Lake Placid as well.

If the term had existed then, the twins would have been called jocks, since, according to Margie, "When my mum was twenty-four, she thought everyone woke up at five or six in the morning and waxed their skis! She was a sports person. That's what she did. That's what *they* did."

After the Olympics, the twins celebrated a double wedding in Montreal in 1948: Rhona to Gene Gillis and Rhoda to Arnold Eaves. Then Gene and Rhona moved to Whitefish, Montana, where they ran a ski school and ski shop. Rhona gave birth to four children in six years. But then the marriage disintegrated. She and the four kids returned to Montreal, and, according to Gillis, though her father did pay some child support, he disappeared "quite radi-cally from our lives":

> We all lived together in a very small apartment. Not much money, lots of pressure. When my father divorced her, she was basically ostracized from her community. She was a young, single woman, vivacious, and none of her peer group wanted her around anymore. She was kind of dangerous, they thought. At one point, her church group tried to say she couldn't belong to it

because she was divorced. She was going through a lot, and she loved my father deeply. She was distraught, and I really resented her pain, didn't want her to be in pain.

Rhona Gillis strapped on her skis and started teaching skiing at what she called the Ski Jay Ski School in the Laurentian Mountains. She supported her four kids and never remarried. One of her favorite sayings, according to Margie, is, "'Well, something has to be done. Who's going to do it?' That kind of dig-in-ness and that courage that it took to deal with life on a sort of very practical level was to do it, just get the thing done, no matter how impossible it seemed."

According to Margie, her mother always said she was a difficult birth. There were complications, and her mother had to be hospitalized afterward. Margie remembers that she was "not an easy child. And that is one of the first things I've heard all my life: 'You were trouble since the word go.'" But her mother believed in her and she is grateful for that.

Today, at seventy-four, Rhona and Rhoda still run a ski school in the Laurentians for housewives where, according to Margie, "the hours are such that you could put your kids in school, tear up to the Laurentians, ski, and get back in time for your kids. So a lot of women joined this; they got their sense of identity and strength here." It is fittingly called the Twinski Club, and Rhona and Rhoda take their students to other challenging ski trails. In 1995, they escorted one-third of their members (all in their seventies) to Chamonix, France. Occasionally they bungee jump or "parapont," which Margie describes as a combination of skiing and parachuting.

Rhona lives in her father's old estate outside Montreal and still works at "making do," as she has always advised her daughter she should. Sometimes this means Margie will arrive and find her mother (and Rhoda on occasion) attempting to chop down a tree with carving knives. Other times, Rhona will climb to the third story of the house to install the storm windows, though several years ago she fell on her back and later required surgery. Had she called the doctor? Margie asked. "No dear, don't worry. I've just taken an aspirin, and I'll be fine" was the answer.

In one of her favorite pieces, "When the Rosehips Quiver," Margie portrays a young girl impatiently waiting to be asked to dance, all the while perched uncomfortably on a chair. She's dressed in a most ladylike pink dress with a sash and has her hands folded as she waits for a young man to ask her onto the floor. Young fiddling sensation Ashley McIsaac, from Nova Scotia, plays his instrument furiously as Margie looks right and left for a partner. She's tapping her feet and banging her heels, and her dress is flipping indecorously around; as she gets into the music, the dress flips over her head. Eventually, Gillis, without partner but with much gusto, gets up and dances a wild gig, and her fiddler encourages this act of independence. Exhausted at the finale, she falls on her derriere to the floor. This independence seems quite appropriate for the daughter of a trailblazer like Rhona—one of a kind, braving the dance floor even in her mid-forties, when most other dancers would have retired to the sidelines.

Margie Gillis remembers her mother's advice: "'If you can't fall down, you can't stand up.' And I apply that to everything in my life. Everything, everything, everything. And she was very practical about it on a physical, kinetic level, in her teaching us how to fall down. We were applauded for having a good fall, a scraped knee. I use that to teach dancing, to celebrate this. How you fall is good and how you recover is important. Oh my gosh, it's exciting."

Margie Gillis and Sandra Rivers are just two of the millions of baby boomer women born in North America to mothers who would have liked to live the life they saw in *Ladies' Home Journal,* but who carved out something quite different because circumstances dictated they do so. Mrs. Rivers and Mrs. Gillis did not think they were inventing a theory of raising daughters counter to that embraced by society and by child psychologists at the time—which generally resulted in daughters who were likely to follow traditional paths. These mothers found a deep strength to carry on in spite of being single mothers with limited incomes, and they instilled that strength in their daughters. Their daughters' successes as solo artists in fields where achievement is rare and financial rewards even rarer are a testimony to this great gift.

Just Wait Until You Have Children of Your Own

We are both mothers now. That changed everything for me.

> Sally, thirty-nine-year-old optometric
> assistant and mother of two from Colorado

She was always there when I needed her, even lying for me to the attendance office when I cut school. She was mad as hell, but protected me.

> Kristine, forty-two-year-old
> sales representative from Arizona

Given the two very disparate worlds baby boomer daughters and our mothers live in, it has been especially difficult to relate to each other sometimes. A daughter who is going through a divorce and negotiating maintenance payments and battling issues related to custody might be more likely to seek the support and advice from a woman who has been through a divorce rather than her mom who has not. Kristine is one of these women; she says, "Because I'm divorced, I was faced with problems she never, ever had to face! She's been married to the same man for forty-nine years. I will never have that in my lifetime. Our differences stem from her never having walked in my shoes."

That is not to say that some daughters, particularly the Untraveled ones, might not seek support, comfort, and advice from their

81

moms in these situations. However, whether they actually heed mom's advice depends on how realistic her guidance is. Lainie, a forty-nine-year-old mother of two from Connecticut, just recently abandoned by her husband for a younger woman, says, "My mom has been terrific since my husband left. As soon as I could, I moved nearer to her. She's been great to me and the kids, really helping me until I get on my feet financially. But whenever I vent my anger or when I just break down and cry because I feel so overwhelmed, she just won't listen. She insists I get on with my life and bite the bullet! Easy for her to say. She's never been left with two kids and no money coming in. I decided to join a divorced and separated group from the local church. At least there I'll be able to get the support I need from women who've walked in my shoes."

Walking in corporate "shoes" is something most of our moms have not had to do in their lifetimes either. So when a daughter is the victim of sexual harassment from a boss who will determine her career path within the company, she will seek the advice of another woman, one familiar with corporate politics, as opposed to going to her mom, whose only job experience has been that of a housewife or a few erratic part-time positions.

We Are One

And so we each often feel awkward and uncomfortable when we travel in those parts of each other's worlds that are foreign to us—until we become mothers, that is. Giving birth initiates us into our mothers' world. Motherhood brings us back to them and can make a significant difference in our relationship, as in the case of Mindy, a self-employed mother of one, who says, "Having my son brought my mother and me closer since we have together raised him and are always doing things together. She is left-handed, and my son is left-handed, so their motor skills are on the same level, and she could help him with that particular challenge. She has always reassured me about my son and his personality and character. Without her wisdom, I would have been lost."

For many of us, motherhood serves as a bridge to greater intimacy with our moms. Tamara, a thirty-nine-year-old married mother of two from Ohio, who works full-time as a consumer researcher, says of her mom, "When I was expecting my first child, it was the first time my mother opened up to me on what life was like for her as a young woman." Tamara's mom, seventy-four, mother of ten, had an eighth-grade education and returned to work when Tamara was four-teen years old. She worked two jobs, as a janitor and as a cleaning woman.

Margot, a mother of four, whose own mom raised five children while working at various odd jobs, also talks of the shift in their relationship: "My mom and I never had talks and sharing times until after I started having babies."

For some daughters, becoming a mother gives them a new slant on their moms. Marilyn, an office manager and mother of two from Ohio, says, "I understand more about the stresses of being a mother since I am one. Now that I have lived some years and suffered some pain and had children, I think she respects me more than she used to. She treats me better now."

Sandra Bezic, Choreographer and Mother

Sandra Bezic, producer of Stars on Ice and a former Canadian champion skater, has served as choreographer for such skating stars as Kurt Browning, Kristi Yamaguchi, Ekaterina Gordeeva, Katarina Witt, and legendary pairs' skaters Barbara Underhill and Paul Mar-tini. Brian Boitano won the 1988 Olympics Gold Medal with much assistance from Sandra, who gave his skating a new life and creative punch with her choreography, allowing him to win by a hair over the reigning world champion, Brian Orser.

The world of figure skating gave Sandra Bezic and her mother a common dream, but it was not until Sandra gave birth to her son, Dean, that their relationship took on another dimension.

Bezic's mother, Angeline, and her father, Dusan, were born in Croatia, on an island in the Adriatic off the city of Split. Growing up, Angeline saw Norway's Sonja Henie skate her way through 20th Century Fox movies like *Sun Valley Serenade* and was inspired. Sandra thinks this experience sits at the base of her mother's ambitions for her as a skater. She and her brother, Val, began lessons at an early age. Together they won their first senior Canadian title when she was thirteen and won an additional four during the next five years. Certainly it is true that Sandra saw the world, but it was in a whirl and all under the enormous stress that presses down on competitive figure skaters.

Although their love for skating has been a major area of connection in the relationship between Sandra and her mother, it has also served as a major source of tension. "It was always the push, the push, the push, always the push," says Bezic. "And I needed that push. It was good, not like some I've seen. But still, I had to sort it out. That's why I had a really tough time in my late teens." Sandra could not take the pressure and the life she found herself looking at, so she quit. She opened up a café in the trendy Yorkville district in Toronto, hoping to find herself and who she was apart from her skates and her mother's dream.

After several years away from the ice, Sandra "decided if I was going to do something for ten hours a day, it might as well be something I enjoyed, that maybe I have a talent for. A friend prompted me, pushed me. So I decided and made a conscious decision to get back into figure skating. But I did not want to have a traditional role or be a traditional coach."

Sandra says that her mother still wants her to perform: "She'd still be happiest if I were out there in the spotlight, but the next best thing is choreography. I think she's intrigued by the directing, producing, and all that stuff—but far more interested in my performing than in my choreography."

Sandra's relationship with her mother, like all other mother-daughter relationships, is a work in progress. Her newest career as a mom has added another dimension to her relationship with her mother: "I think things are changing. I think my son's made a huge difference. I think she's really found pleasure in him and found pleasure in watching me with him, and I really want her to be happy. So I do think that maybe in a way I'm winning approval." As she says this, her face brightens with a huge smile.

Sandra is finally winning approval for something her mom can truly relate to. Her skating career has been only a dream and vicarious experience for her mom. Mothering, on the other hand, is an experience she has lived.

The shared experience of motherhood can bring a new energy to the mother-daughter relationship and develop fertile ground for a deeper connection. This is not to say that daughters without children cannot move to a deeper connection with their moms as well. These mothers and daughters without the focus of grandchildren can, if they choose, spend more energy on developing other common interests. (Our survey did not address this particular issue, but we noted no great difference in responses between those women who had children and those who did not.)

The Lessons Taught

With the onset of our motherhood, our moms' career deficits no longer serve as a wedge between us. The mentoring our mothers offer us comes by way of not only what they did well but equally, and sometimes even more powerfully, by what they did *not* do so well. Poor mothering, even abusive mothering, can serve as an impetus and baseline for how *not* to mother. Learning by our mothers' mistakes is something Untraveled and Prodigal Daughters are talented at doing. Wandering Daughters have a greater challenge in this process.

The parenting wisdom and advice offered both directly and indirectly that our respondents and interviewees most valued generally dealt with issues of patience, boundaries, unconditional love, communication, and self-sacrifice.

Patience

Many of our respondents commented that their moms taught them how to be patient. Rose, a homemaker, part-time librarian, and mother of three from Illinois, says, "When I was a new mom with a very troublesome infant, she told me to think of the willow trees outside the window and bend like they do. At the time, I was extremely perfectionistic and inflexible. It was something I could visualize that helped me relax my mind, body, and behavior."

For Blanche, learning patience from her physically and verbally abusive mother was achieved through hard work and persistence and was accomplished by focusing on managing her own anger. A married mother of two teenagers who works as a personal care aide, Blanche says, "I don't ever want to be verbally and physically abusive the way she was. I've learned to have patience, understanding, and love when dealing with my daughters. I try to stay away from the negative feelings."

The issue of patience can be a real challenge to those of us who are single working moms. The stresses and strains of our jobs and the struggles to make ends meet often leave little in the way of patience for our children. One of our respondents, a forty-eight-year-old financial planner and married mother of two, feels "so stretched by the time dinner is over that I often find myself snapping at my kids and just wanting to kick the dog! I often think of my mom and how patient she was with me. Even though she didn't have to work, I know I can learn from her example. So when I'm particularly frayed, I just think of her. The image of her face helps to increase my patience with my own kids."

Boundaries

Given that our moms' energies were narrowly focused on child rearing, some of our respondents' moms encouraged their daughters to be wary of letting their relationship with their children adversely affect their marriage. Our moms know how easy it is to let children slip into the space left by husbands who become increasingly immersed in their work, a world alien to them. Linda, a magazine production manager from British Columbia and mother of one newborn child, says, "My parents always maintained that the primary relationship in the family was between them and that women should not let children usurp husbands. My parents have a very strong relationship, and I think this made for a healthy family unit. It gave us independence, and it underscored their superlative respect for each other."

In addition to their cautionary advice about boundaries in protecting our marital relationships, a good many of our moms also warned us not to suffocate our children. Beverly's mom taught her "how to give my son his freedom, to let him have his own life and not to smother him with my focused love." For the majority of our respondents and interviewees, however, this boundary issue was communicated more by what our mothers did not do.

Self-Esteem and Control

The development and formation of clear boundaries between a parent and a child is greatly influenced by the mother's self-esteem. Since our moms' energies were expended primarily on rearing children, their self-esteem was determined in large part by how well their little darlings turned out. Getting their children to serve as benchmarks of their success was a herculean task and one that generally failed miserably because any good behavior or achievement was easily eclipsed by the simplest wrongdoing or failure. And as we got older, the stakes got higher. Dealing with the negligence of a child who does not say "please" or "thank you" in front of Grandma is small potatoes in comparison to a teen pregnancy or a failed marriage. Our mothers' self-esteem needs sometimes became a bottomless pit, which fostered anger and frustration on their part and ours. Since they had few other avenues to offset their jobs as moms and since their contributions to society were greatly devalued (highlighted by the fact that time spent on homemaking was and still is not included in the official measures of national output such as the

GNP), they inadvertently continued to try even harder to fill the sinkhole of their self-esteem through their children, making us the focus of their lives. The boundaries between us became flimsier and fuzzier. And for those who worked outside the home, their jobs, erratic and part-time for the most part, were not acquired as a means to fulfill their potential, but rather to earn extra income or for sheer survival if divorce or death of a spouse was a factor. Thus our moms, whether or not they worked outside the home, generally looked to us as the greatest source of personal fulfillment. When asked to rank their moms' self-esteem, 64 percent of our respondents whose moms were primarily homemakers felt it was low, with 18 percent reporting it as average and only 18 percent ranking it as high.

Thus, given what was on the line, some of our moms, especially stay-at-home moms, had a tough time letting us make mistakes. After all, what would other people think? This question was frequently asked, although never in its entirety. Secretly, we both knew and carried the burden of the unspoken words: What would other people think . . . of her as a mother? And so some of our moms became controlling, overprotective, and manipulative. Maureen, a single legal secretary, says of her mom, "My mother didn't give me any control over my personal life or much freedom. I'll raise my children very differently. I'll let them make many more of their own choices and not be as overprotective and controlling." Maureen's mom was primarily a homemaker with a sprinkling of some erratic part-time jobs.

They were controlling and overprotective, all in the name of a mother's love. And it was love—the love of women whose lives were constricted to a very narrow space of their potential. Consider Cassie, a forty-nine-year-old married mother of two from Red Deer, Alberta—a Prodigal Daughter who had a very strained relationship with her mother who, although a registered nurse, remained a homemaker after marriage. She shares how her mom's controlling parenting style has taught her about boundaries:

My mother was extremely controlling, and I allowed her to be. There was a great deal of tension in the house. Mother and Dad weren't close, and my sister, born with a very aggressive personality, took a very oppositional role to the amount of control demanded. It served as an example to me in my own parenting style to try to be flexible and to value my children's differences. I make a conscious effort not to manipulate with guilt and silences. I am very aware of seeking balance between order and obsessiveness. It is really important for me to be close to them, so I have to give them some privacy and space so that closeness is a choice, not an obligation. I try to reach balance in all things, their wants, needs, and mine for them.

In looking at what her mother gave her, she says, "I must have learned my capacity for love from my mother, but maybe experiencing the darker side of it, I learned that it's not something you have, then take for granted. It takes examination and commitment. I'm sure Mother thought she loved her children passionately, without realizing she put conditions on it. I try very hard to love my children openly and expressively and without conditions. I also learned that you won't lose someone because you don't control them."

Those moms whose worlds went beyond their children seemed less controlling, less likely needing them to fill their self-esteem needs. The boundaries between parent and child were clearer and more well defined. Betty, a forty-year-old attorney and a married mother of one, says, "As my children grow, I hope I'll be able to let them make their own mistakes without making it worse. I remember when I dyed my brown hair red at age fourteen, and it turned bright orange in the sunshine. My mother said nothing. I've never colored my hair again."

Mae, whose mom was an assistant comptroller of a company and an accountant for forty-seven years, shares her experience: "While my mother holds strong opinions, she is nonjudgmental and respectful of my decisions. I have tried to give this same gift to my daughter: the strong support of love and trust, yet the freedom to grow, make mistakes, risk and try again."

Unconditional Love

Unconditional love is at the heart of motherhood and assumed to be a given. Defining this term is a bit tricky since everyone has an idea of what it means. Does it mean always putting someone else first? Or does it mean always being there, no matter what? Or does it mean respecting differences and personal space and being able to communicate freely and openly, conflicts and all, without fear of judgment or rejection? Or maybe it means forgiveness, so that no matter what crimes have been committed against the relationship, there is always a pardon? Or does it mean what it does to modern dancer Margie Gillis? "I get to go home, and she tells me what a great daughter I am. 'Oh my God. Look! Not only does she dance, she washes dishes!' I adore it. I want that. I want that absolute unconditional love. I love going home. I'm tired. I'm just a mess. And my mummy tells me I'm wonderful. I'm gorgeous and beautiful. And in that I can do no wrong."

Based on our data, the one type of unconditional love that most of our respondents and interviewees describe having received from their moms and one type they were most influenced by is best described by a forty-five-year-old administrative secretary in Colorado, married, and the mother of one teenager, who says: "The one value my mom passed along to me that I would like to pass along to my children is to always let your children know that they can 'come home.' That you will be there for them. The unconditional love thing."

For some of us whose moms were housewives, this quality of "thereness" was in part made easier by our moms' ability to be single-minded since their children were their main focus, as in Kristine's case. A divorced mother of one from Arizona, she says of her mom, "I always knew that (and still know now) my mother was always there for me, no matter how much she disagreed with me, or was angry with me. She always came through. She was devoted to her family totally. She didn't work, so she focused on us—my sister, my dad, and me. She was always there when I needed her, even lying for me to the attendance office when I cut school. She was mad as hell, but protected me."

For those of us whose moms were divorced and/or employed, being there was more of a challenge. Jeanelle, a thirty-seven-year-old engineer and mother of two, says her mom "always put us kids first. When she was a young woman, she was a working mom when most others weren't. She had no activities outside of work that didn't involve us kids. I've done the exact same thing."

For many of our respondents and interviewees, the unconditional love from our moms was rarely diminished by the hardships they faced in their lives, as with Julie, a thirty-six-year-old sales representative and a single mother of three from Illinois. Her mom, abandoned by her husband and with an eleventh-grade education, had to work in various clerical and customer service jobs, factories, bars, and hotels to support her family of eight children, four of whom are now deceased: "My mother has influenced me a lot in parenting. She was an open, kind mother who would help her children any way possible. I never felt like my mother wished I'd go somewhere else! To this day, every time I enter her house, I know that I'm safe, and if I'm having a bad day, I always feel better, secure, and stronger just having been with her or talked with her. I hope that my children feel these same ways as I feel about my mother."

Wandering Daughters and some Prodigal Daughters may have difficulty recognizing any unconditional love in their relationships with their moms, which is often due to accumulated feelings of anger and resentments. Crystal, a forty-two-year-old corporate trainer, divorcée and mother of one from Illinois, says:

The woman is my mother, and because of that, I feel
some affinity. But honestly, ours is the most substandard
relationship in my life. I have many wonderful relationships in my life. I have come to learn what unconditional love feels like. I did not, however, learn this at her
knee. I don't feel as if we ever bonded. In many ways, our
relationship has taught me what not to do in the name
of love. In many ways, I am stronger and more capable
as a woman because of it. My mother is not the kind of
person I would choose to have in my life. I find it best to
limit our contact.

Crystal has learned about unconditional love inversely from her
mom. Crystal's mom, mother to four, suffered severe agoraphobia,
leaving Crystal, the oldest daughter, to assume responsibilities for
the family.

Communication

If our mothers' self-esteem was at all shaky, the quality of our communications with them was most likely to be affected. And although many of our respondents and interviewees felt that the level
of communication with their moms was often fairly superficial, there
were degrees to this superficiality. Some boomer daughters, usually
the Untraveled ones, were able to be somewhat more open with
their feelings and less secretive about their activities. Although several factors could account for this (one of them self-esteem), it is
clear that these moms did not tend to personalize the information
shared as their success or failure. Kate, a physical therapist and
mother of one from California, says her "mom was nonjudgmental,
and she taught me to be a good listener. This really helped me do
the right things when my daughter was a teenager. I never let anything my daughter said shock me, so communication stayed open."

Communicating our feelings, thoughts, and opinions openly,
without fear of jeopardizing the relationship or injuring our moms'

self-esteem, is what the majority of boomer daughters want most of all. And for those of us who could not have it with our moms, we wanted to make sure we had it with our kids, as one Wandering Daughter, a financial coordinator from California, says: "My mother was very strict, so I vowed I would never be that way with my children. I wanted open and honest communication, not just giving speeches when she would say she loved me but didn't really mean it." Jennifer, who holds an M.B.A. and is the mother of one, says of her mom, who was a full-time homemaker, "My mother never listened or really talked with me, so I concentrate on communication with my daughter, bolstering her ego and encouraging her to make decisions." Margot, mother of four, says, "If I give advice now to my kids, we sit and talk things through and exchange ideas."

And if we, by virtue of ignorance or laziness, continue the pattern, our daughters will often shake us out of our lethargy by teasing or taunting us about how "weird" we are when we are around Grandma. They know something is amiss, and they do not want our relationship to mirror what they observe between their grandmas and us. Carol Ann, a teacher's aide and substitute teacher, married mother of two, says, "My daughter sees how I am with my mom and hopes it won't be that way with us. My daughter and I talk openly about our feelings, and she'll tell me if she feels I'm intruding in her privacy. She is in her twenties. I think if I had done this when I was her age, I wouldn't be resenting my mom so much now."

Sex Talk

There were some topics that were more taboo than others, and S-E-X headed the list. When it came to boys (and, later, men), dating, and sex, let's be honest: in dealing with us, our moms were less than prepared. As one of our respondents says, "I don't think my parents had much of a sex life. Sometimes I wonder how I was conceived." There is no doubt that they were operating at a handicap, given that many of them learned little, if anything, from their own mothers. Plus, there was no Oprah in the afternoon to bolster their information base on sex and dating. For them, it became a learning-by-doing experience. With this in mind, we got the best of what they were capable of giving us, which would not give them an A on the Masters and Johnson scoring card. (Actually, they would do well to get a C.) For many of them, their first class in sex education took place on their wedding night. In addition, they were victims of the cultural hypnosis that continued to vilify the female sex drive outside of marriage.

Although there were a few who commented that their moms communicated openly and positively about sex, like Janis, whose mom taught her that "sex is natural and fun and pleasurable," the vast majority of our respondents remarked that their moms' comments about sex were negative. A thirty-seven-year-old paramedic from Ohio is typical: "My mother taught me that sex was something to be ashamed of . . . that my sexual organs were nasty. However, this was not spoken but implied."

The most common method our mothers used to communicate about sex, dating, and men was offered via clichés and homilies, as with Lillian, a paramedic from Ohio, who says sex was something she and her mom would not discuss openly and that when the topic was broached, her mother would resort to the sound bites of clichés: "'Boys want to be with girls for one thing only.' 'Nice girls don't do that.' It really screwed up my self-concept. I was a sexual being and still am. But for many years I thought I was 'dirty' for liking sex, for wanting it, for exploring my sexuality. I thought there was something wrong with me and that I was a 'bad girl.'"

For the most part, our mothers taught a simple arithmetic equation when it came to sex. If we put out, we would lose, which underscored the law of diminishing returns. Colette, a mother of four from Illinois, says, "My mother's perspective on this from the beginning—and still today—is that men want only one thing from women, and that's sex. And through sex, they diminish women as having any value." Another respondent says her mother taught her to "use sex as a weapon." Our teenage daughters would find this advice most amusing.

The pressure to behave in public as well as private in accordance with these standards is the reason that so many of our mothers said, "Behave like a lady!" Rhonda remembers her mother scolding her after seeing a young couple amorously embracing each other: "'Don't you ever do that. You should never do anything with a boy that you wouldn't do in front of your father or me.' She made me feel as if affection and sexuality were wrong, dirty, not healthy. I think I experienced a lot of unnecessary guilt, and I made some less than wise choices in some relationships and sexual encounters."

Obviously this advice was one-sided. This is what Carrie sees, now at the age of forty-five, as she assesses her mom's counsel on sex:

> One of my mother's shortcomings was her lack of frank-
> ness about sex and how wonderful it could be as well as
> how terrible it could be under the wrong circumstances.
> As well, her unwillingness to guide me in these matters
> and her screwed-up 'men are not okay' attitudes also hurt
> me. I think it took me a long time to get comfortable
> with my physical, sexual self, to recognize a good male-
> female relationship from a bad one.

And even when they were able to muster up the courage to discuss sex, they often did so by way of aphorisms: "Nice girls don't." "Boys only want one thing." "He won't buy the cow if he gets the milk for free." These sound bites, which were frequently coated with threatening undertones, were often used tactically to instill shame, guilt, and fear within us. These were often the only weapons our moms had in the war against raging adolescent hormones and their offshoot, pregnancy.

Breaking Free

These homilies and other brief and succinct views on sex passed on to us did not allow for much in the way of discussion, questions and answers, and the sort of thing we expect our teenage daughters to engage us in. Nevertheless, our mothers' messages were powerful, albeit subtle, and at the same time let them off the hook when it came to a full briefing about men and sex.

According to our survey respondents, in ranking relationships with boys as teenagers, 31 percent said their mothers had a positive influence in this area, 36 percent said it was negative, and 33 percent said their mother had no influence. Thus, despite all the noise, about a third of us tuned our moms out.

In spite of all of our criticisms and complaints as to how our moms screwed us up when it came to sex and our sexuality, it appears as though our barks are worse than our bites. Fewer than half (45 percent) of our respondents say their mom's influence on their sexuality was negative during their adolescence, while 19 percent of our respondents say they were positively influenced by their moms, and 36 percent say their moms had no influence. As adults, only 15 percent say their mom's influence was negative, 21 percent say their moms had a positive influence, and 63 percent say their moms had no influence on their sexuality. It seems as though the majority of boomer daughters have carved out a sexuality unique to their own needs and value systems.

Sex and Our Daughters

Even as liberal as boomer daughters are, some of us have difficulty being open with our daughters about their sexuality, but we are determined not to repeat the pattern. Sally, the mother of two teenagers and an optometric assistant, says her mom "never spoke to me of sex, which is something I was determined to be very open with my kids about, and I am. It's not easy, but worth my occasional bouts with uncomfortableness."

In working with adolescent females and their moms, I (BMc) have been particularly struck by the candid conversations that take place in my office. Initially, girls still display a degree of caution about revealing their sexual activities to their moms. However, when their mothers discover that they *are* sexually active and the shock waves subside (usually rather quickly), the discussions between the two are fairly open and filled with talk about birth control, sexually transmitted diseases, and values related to sexual decision making. And all of this is usually done without the use of aphorisms. However, if the daughter does not show the proper amount of maturity in these discussions and the mother is feeling desperate in trying to punctuate a particular point, there have been a few "cows" and "free milk" thrown in (if nothing else, it adds a little levity).

Given today's world, with rising alcohol, tobacco, and drug use and sexual activity among teenagers, our kids have to make tough decisions that go far beyond what we faced. Maintaining open lines of communication within a relationship of trust and respect is an absolute necessity for us as parents today. Although our faces are lined with anxiety and worry, we want our kids to have few secrets from us . . . most of the time.

There was one boomer mother of an eighteen-year-old daughter I worked with who was particularly proud of the honest and open relationship she had with her daughter—the exact opposite of her own relationship with her mom. In discussing these relationships at one of our sessions, she said, "You know, I came home from work early the other day and found my daughter and her boyfriend in her bedroom having sex! I was so upset. I would have NEVER done that. I still feel uncomfortable having sex with my HUSBAND at my mother's house. So I told my daughter that if she wanted to have sex, that was her decision. But she needed to be a little sneaky about it . . . like I was when I was her age."

And so in a strange, oblique way, perhaps some of our mothers' greatest gifts to us were the silences and the unexpressed feelings, the forbidden topics that characterized the communication between us. These serve as the spark that ignites a deeper connection with our children, drawing them nearer to us. And so, even though most of us frequently still have to strain across a vast chasm filled with feelings of discomfort and embarrassment to communicate at a deeper level with our moms, we can gain some comfort in knowing

that there is much less of a space between our children and ourselves because of it.

Broken Eggs

Although the locations and the players may vary, many of us share
a common memory when it comes to our moms. It might take place
on a Saturday or Sunday morning. Our dads could be plopped in
front of a black-and-white TV screen, comfortably embraced by the
tattered arms of their La-Z-Boy chair, newspapers scattered at their
feet. Our brothers and sisters might be lying belly up, not too far
from the strewn papers caught between our dad's rather large feet,
playing with the dog or cat while we were engrossed in what our
Revlon doll will wear to her next party. All the while, the odors of
bacon and eggs permeate the air and tease at our nostrils. Our moms
are scurrying around the kitchen—a rather small, cramped room
with no microwave, dishwasher, or Teflon-coated pans. They are a
bit ticked off that their daughters are not helping them in spite of
persistent pleading. They call loudly for everyone to come to the
table. As we all settle into our usual places, she reminds us with
some irritation and an icy glance, to get up and help her, com-
manding us to get the orange juice or the milk or perhaps to retrieve
the toast, which no one will want given the burned smell that is
emanating from the toaster. So we surreptitiously slip two more
pieces of bread in.

As she serves breakfast, she accidentally breaks the yolk of one
of the eggs: "Oh, shoot. Well, I'll take that one." And contrary to
the usual serving order, which puts Dad and the boys at the forefront, she serves herself first and places the damaged egg carelessly
on her plate. And when the sizzling bacon or greasy sausage is being
delivered at her hands, she takes the smallest or the most shriveled
piece. And of course, she reaches for the burned toast.

Yes, broken eggs are common to most of us and epitomize the
self-sacrifice that characterized our mothers' lives. And as mothers

now, we know that motherhood and self-sacrifice are constant companions, as inseparable as bread and butter. Our moms not only taught us about patience, communication, and boundaries, but also about self-sacrifice. This, however, is the lesson we have struggled with the most.

Many of our respondents and interviewees commented on the sacrifices made by their moms. While Jeanine's mom raised five children, she supported the family by "cleaning houses and taking in ironing." In talking about her mom, Jeanine, a divorced waitress from California, says, "I am now more aware of the sacrifices my mom made for me. And when I see some of the ways my girlfriends raise their kids, I'm now grateful for a lot of the traits my mother instilled in me, like respect for others, punctuality. Even though my mom and I disagree on many issues, I believe more often that she does the best she knows how." (Jeanine has no children.)

And yet it was this very self-sacrifice that propelled us to make sure we had different, more fulfilling lives than our mothers had. The sacrifices they made placed them in a very vulnerable, dependent economic position, which kept them powerless and garnered them little recognition or appreciation. More important, for many of our moms, this self-sacrifice snuffed out any sense of a self apart from the family. Janet, a mother of three, says:

> My mother has very little sense of self. Her life is her family; she always put herself last on the list; everyone else's needs and desires come first and are met at her expense. She waits on her family hand and foot. She still does things for my father and brother that they were capable of doing at eight years old. This was my norm, my role model, of a good wife and mother and caused much conflict and anguish for me when I couldn't be happy doing the same things. I never developed a sense of self. I buried my own needs under those of my family.

At What Cost?

In talking about her mom's self-sacrifice, Celeste, a divorced mother of three from Colorado, asks the question most often asked by boomer daughters: At what cost?

> Since my mother placed wife, mother, and church worker above all else, I've weighed my own experience as well as the knowledge of women's issues I've gained against her values. At times, I felt she's been sold a bill of goods not worthy of her. At times, I've seen how her self-sacrifice allowed others to benefit. I've often compared the wife-mother role to that of slaves. It benefits greatly those around, but at what cost to the woman? I now wish I could have more flexibility to be a mother and homemaker without breadwinning interfering, but I also couldn't give up my power and freedom that money allows. Balancing my life within societal constraints remains hard.

We are continually striving to make sure our kids can have even more than we had. We work extra hours to get a promotion or take on additional clients in order to earn more money—money so that our kids can go to the best schools, wear the hottest labels, be involved in everything from soccer to band—but at what cost to the woman?

When it came to our after-school activities, our moms enrolled us in one or two at the most, like ballet or Brownies, which were generally within a bike ride's distance. Moms today are carting their kids to multiple sports activities, gymnastics, and dance classes, the majority of which are on opposite sides of town. If there is any kind of public transportation, it is not safe or reliable or frequent enough.

Or our kids want us to be their chauffeurs, and we oblige. One woman reported that given the activities her three kids are involved in, they rarely sit down to dinner at all. Everyone eats on the run.

A thirty-nine-year-old mother of three girls analyzes the frenetic pace we are living: "You know, we're shoving our kids out on the superhighway and not letting them enjoy the scenic country roads! Whatever happened to just coming home from school, grabbing a snack, and then going for a bike ride or playing hopscotch or even reading together?"

Juggling project deadlines with kids' dental appointments and soccer games is wearing thin. Battling in the trenches all day at work and then facing the tasks related to maintaining the troops at home—last-minute grocery shopping, cooking dinner or picking up fast food on the way to the cleaners, homework duty, and refereeing sibling rivalry—leaves little energy for much else. In addition, women are more burdened than their spouses by housework. Recent studies estimate that representative values of housework time range around six to fourteen hours per week for men and twenty to thirty hours per week for women. All of these responsibilities put a strain on the free time we have with our kids, let alone with our husbands. It is difficult to be patient, charming, and sexy when we can barely drag our weary bodies upstairs to bed.

So how can we even dare to think of any free time for ourselves for simple things like reading a book, or taking an uninterrupted walk or hot bath, or of getting our own needs met? Time for ourselves and the energy to fill it is as precious as moon ice. All of these demands on our time are exacerbated for single moms and moms of blended families, where dealing with stepchildren add to the overload.

Slaves with Different Masters

The most ubiquitous lesson of motherhood learned at our mothers' knees has to do with self-sacrifice. At first glance, it appears to have taken on a new and different face for boomer daughters, especially since our lives are a reflection of our unwillingness to sacrifice our potential as our moms did. Upon closer scrutiny, however, it is clear that many of us actually are clones of our mothers in this department; we are slaves but with different masters.

Our moms were slaves to their limited options: being economically dependent, trapped in a marriage due to a lack of financial and personal resources, serving as handmaids to their family's needs, using children as a source of self-esteem. We, on the other hand, have become greater slaves because of our increased options. Boomer daughters have a much more frantic, harried pace than our moms did. Life seems to be harder and more demanding, generating feelings of overwhelming exhaustion and feelings of discontent. Although the Virginia Slims ad touts that we have come a long way, the model depicted does not capture how frayed and frazzled we often feel as a result of having achieved this dubious feat.

I (BMc) can remember my mom, a housewife, religiously watched *As The World Turns* and *General Hospital*, and my sister and I knew better than to disturb her. Sometimes in the middle of the day, she would take a twenty-minute snooze on the couch. In spite of her many homemaking responsibilities, which were not made easier by microwaves, dishwashers, and the like, she was able to carve time out, if only a few minutes, for herself. A working mother today would think she entered the Twilight Zone if she found herself with an unused space of time in which no demands were placed on her. Having options has been both a blessing and a curse, as well as a seduction that keeps us believing we should be fulfilled.

As a psychologist, I work with a large number of boomer women who report symptoms of depression and a vague inner dissatisfaction. I am struck by the schedules women keep and the people they care for; the range is phenomenal and often includes children, aging parents and in-laws, pets, employees, friends, and neighbors. The one pattern that emerges over and over again is the inability of my clients to nurture themselves amid this potpourri of human beings.

An Oxymoron: Selfish Women

These women, constantly torn between significant others and work, always worrying about one while involved with the other, have difficulty allowing for any space between the two—space where their needs are met, where they take care of themselves and decompress. Anytime they step into this space, if and when they even know to do so, their guilt squeezes them back out.

The majority of the counseling I do primarily focuses on two issues: self-care skills and diffusing the guilt associated with these activities. Many of my clients cannot tolerate the thought of being "selfish." It is almost as though selfishness were a dreaded disease. Although we think we are so very different from our moms because we have careers, in one very subtle but powerful way we are very much afflicted with what we rebelled against in her.

Part of therapy aims toward helping women get comfortable with the notion of being "selfish"—something that our culture will especially not tolerate in women, and even less so in mothers. Using the word *selfish* in therapy is intentional and is used for shock value. By freely and openly talking about "selfishness," women are better able to give themselves permission to begin the process of change, and by becoming desensitized to the "S" word, the women I work with are relieved of the layers of guilt (which have been accumulating in the female collective unconscious for eons) that have burdened them, since they often are unclear about how much to give and how much to take.

Although it takes time, eventually they come to realize that by taking care of themselves first, they become even better at giving to others. By taking time out and replenishing themselves through activities such as exercise, meditating, or reading, or by clearly communicating their needs to others, these women are experiencing a new vitality amid their responsibilities. By demanding respect for their time, they are more likely to get it. Ironically, filling these demands (and at first they often have to be demands since our families are resistant to our absences) truly allows for more quality time with kids, spouses, and friends—time where that patience our mothers taught us can flourish.

A few of our respondents commented that they learned self-care the hard way, as did Alice, mother of three from California: "Because my mother put her children and husband first, I let the pendulum swing too far in my own life for a long while. I still think my mom needs to move toward the middle, but I've learned that I don't have to fight to make sure my needs are recognized, that I can take care of my needs in a calmer fashion. I was on the defensive for a long time, expecting people to expect me to put myself last."

Of all the things we learned at our mothers' knees about parenting and motherhood, perhaps the most significant lesson had to do with broken eggs. And although our sense of fair play probably will not allow us to pawn the cracked yolks onto someone else, our new-found "selfishness" will allow us the luxury of frying a new one just for ourselves.

Knowing What to Keep and What to Throw Away

And so as we have faced the challenge of being mothers ourselves, we have had to scrutinize our mothers as mothers ever more closely since it was at their knees that we learned the skills of mothering. And while Untraveled Daughters might be less inclined to find fault with their mother's parenting skills, Wandering Daughters have vowed that they would never, ever be the kind of mother they had. For example, Wendy, the mother of one from Texas, "decided very early on that my mother was a poor parent; I swore that I would learn from what I hated so much in her parenting style." Another respondent from Missouri, a physician's assistant and mother of two, says, "I swore I'd never be the parent she was as far as being out of tune with what's going on."

Often this solemn oath propels Wandering Daughters into a reactive and oppositional parenting style, which actually impedes their ability to make rational decisions based on situations rather than emotional ones driven by their anger and resentment at their mothers' parenting failures. This can lead to a rigid, more reactionary style of parenting or even create self-doubt, as it did with Grace, a Ph.D. student and mother of two from Iowa: "I thought my mother wasn't a good mother in that she was too strict and distant. I was very afraid of my own parenting skills. This made me a strict and sometimes distant mother. When I saw this behavior in me, it made me even more unsure of my own parenting abilities. A vicious cycle was set up."

Some daughters have come to the realization that trying too hard to be different from their moms does not work, as with this respondent from California, a teacher and mother of two: "I think I have tried to be a more 'motherly' mother, baking cookies and all, and that certainly hasn't worked for me." Developing our own personal style of mothering is a process in which our own moms can serve as a point of reference but not as an absolute "right" or "wrong" way to be one. Shaping our own motherhood is in many ways a trial-and-error process, which requires risk taking.

Knowing what to keep of our mothers' parenting style and what to throw away can be particularly difficult for Wandering Daughters, as with Chris, who says, "My mom was too strict with me, and so I lied a lot to her about where I was going, who I was going to be with. She loved me so much and worried so much she made us both crazy. That's why I went totally opposite in raising my daughter. I asked her for advice on raising my daughter and I just didn't listen. The 'shoulda's' and the 'coulda's' and the 'woulda's.' I wasn't strict enough on certain matters, and now my daughter is a slob."

And although all parents want to give their children what they did not get, whether it is material things or more hugs and kisses, Wandering Daughters and some Prodigal Daughters do so with a greater intensity and often with an edge of anger and resentment. This same energy could be used in a way to tap into their creativity and unique parenting style, something Untraveled and some Prodigal Daughters are able to do, as in the case of Elizabeth, the mother of one from Illinois:

> Even though all of my physical needs were met, my mom was distant and aloof, someone who really was a stranger to me. Because I was so angry and resentful of the distance between us, I was obsessed with having a closer relationship with my daughter. Because she had so little breathing room, she kept pushing me away. After much turmoil in our relationship, I sought counseling, which helped me understand my mom's upbringing more. That helped me let go of some of my anger, and so I was able to back off and negotiate a more realistic intimacy between my daughter and me. Although it probably was the most difficult thing I ever faced, I was pleasantly surprised at my ability to do this!

Although Prodigal Daughters often take oaths similar to those of Wandering Daughters, they tend to have a more forgiving attitude toward their mothers' deficiencies. This is not to minimize any neglect or abuse suffered at the hands of mothers. Many of the Prodigal Daughters also suffered neglect and abuse; however, the one difference between the two seems to be that the Prodigals are able to step out of the circle of the mother-as-parent/daughter-as-child relationship and move into the woman-to-woman relationship, which allows for more compassion and forgiveness and less judgment. Carrie, an international business broker who was very deliberate about becoming a mother, says:

> My mother always told me how hard it was for her to be a mother. For a long time, I didn't want to be one

because she was strange and abusive in some ways, as well as excellent in some ways. I had to convince myself that I could adopt her good characteristics as a parent and not use her bad ones, which is still a struggle for me. It was scary to me to think I might do some of the things she did to me emotionally to my child, even though I know I am a different person. It was only when I went through therapy that I exorcized some of my demons about my childhood and thought I could be a decent parent. Of course, in retrospect, it is amazing to me that with her background and education, she was able to be as good a parent as she was.

Perhaps what is different between the Prodigals and Wandering Daughters is that the Prodigals, in coming home, are able to separate their moms from their parenting skills and make decisions on those terms. This acceptance ultimately allows the relationship to transcend the ghosts of the past. It paves the way for those boomer daughters who have had abusive or dysfunctional relationships with their moms to develop a sense of pride and self-respect in knowing that they have prevailed in the face of a very difficult childhood; their resiliency has allowed them to become the women they are and the mothers they wished they had and deserved to have.

6

In God,
All Things Are Possible

*I value these lessons from my mother: that there is
a higher order to things and that having values and
sticking to them are strong elements of character. I
have found great strength and comfort in my search
for wisdom and the voice of God.*

Cassie, teacher from Alberta

Most of our respondents—91 percent—filled in the line where
we asked them to describe their religion. Although a handful listed themselves as atheists, and several more called themselves
agnostics, most identified themselves as something, whether it was
"New Thought," "Unhappy Catholic," or "Undecided." According
to these daughters, their mothers' religion was much more traditional and unequivocal.

Our religions changed tremendously as we grew from little girls
with neat braids and starched dresses and something covering our
head, seated quietly while a man in the pulpit passed along his wisdom. As we modified our dress and started wearing slacks and forget-
ting about anything remotely resembling a hat, the man in the pulpit
sometimes changed to the woman delivering the sermon. Female
clergy began to make their appearance, and even the Catholic church
allowed women to take a more active role in the liturgy of the Mass.
Latin gave way to English (or French or Spanish), and, just like the

Protestants, Catholics started singing in church (not just as members of the choir). Now, if we do take ourselves to temple or church or mosque, we want a greater role for ourselves, and we expect our voices to be heard in decision making that affects the church's operations and its pronouncements. And now, if we take a peek inside any church, we would likely see fewer people, and they are dressed more casually than when we grew up. If our kids attend church and we regale them with our memories of hats and dresses and old-style religion, it sounds as foreign to them as our fond reminiscences about the early days of rock 'n' roll, when we wore crinolines and danced to the Shirelles. For their part, some ministers and priests (like some symphony directors) are just glad to have people in the pews, even if they are wearing (egad!) jeans.

Our Definition of "Religious" Changes

In the beginning, the word came down from the man in pulpit, and we were not encouraged to do much doubting. Depending on the religion, there might have been some room to maneuver, but essentially it was a one-way street. Religious instruction, Sunday school, or religious celebrations ensured that our families tended to gather at some place of worship at some point. In 1955, according to the Princeton Religion Research Center, 49 percent of those surveyed had attended church or synagogue in the past seven days. That dropped to 40 percent in 1970 and has regained three percentage points so that in 1995, 43 percent said they had attended services in the past week. The older the respondent, the more likely it is that the person attends, so that the attendance score of those in the age group thirty to forty-nine stood at only 28 percent.

Most religions now confront change and engage in dialogue. The Catholic church, for one, is confronted by large-scale organizations like Catholics for a Free Choice (whose membership includes nuns), which challenges papal teaching on a variety of subjects: priestly celibacy, birth control, women in the priesthood, abortion, and so on. When we were growing up, that would have been considered heresy, and thus grounds for ejection from the church. Now it is part of the rambunctious nature of Catholicism. Although there are no Catholic female priests, women have made strides in laity leadership, and women in other religions are regularly ordained. According to the National Council of Churches, the number of female ministers grew from 5,591 in 1951 to 20,730 in 1986. The Hartford Study of 1996 noted that less than 1 percent of clergy were women in 1910, but that has risen to 10 percent. The authors of the study nevertheless point to a "stained-glass ceiling" limiting women's progress in this field, compared with medicine and law, where women compose 20 and 25 percent of the ranks, respectively.

Nonetheless, a survey of female leadership in religion by *Working Woman* in late 1996 ran a list of impressive achievements for women in religious leadership. Writer Gustav Niebuhr listed 4,443 female Unitarian ministers, 2,080 Congregationalists, and 3,026 Presbyterians. Reform Judaism has ordained 250 female rabbis and Conservative Judaism, 72. (There are no Orthodox female rabbis.)

Our religious beliefs, like the religions to which we belonged to when we were children, have undergone so much change that it seems impossible to think that as young girls, for example, we were given better grades for having memorized the Baltimore Catechism word for word than for truly understanding the theologically challenging concept of the Trinity or the Doctrine of Original Sin. Now, the Sunday missal we use (if we use anything at all) is a stripped-down version of what we used to dog-ear, and conceptual issues play a larger role in teaching Catholic children about the meaning of their religion. Many of us simply slammed the church door shut, and if we attend now, it is not because we would consider missing Sunday mass a sin.

In 1952, 75 percent of Americans thought Christianity was very important in America; only 52 percent did in 1978. In 1957, seven in ten people said religion was increasing its influence in American life versus 14 percent who said it was not important. *Time* magazine vaulted to the forefront when it asked "Is God Dead?" in its April 8, 1966, edition. Those figures were reversed in 1970. Just four years before this survey, John Lennon announced that the Beatles were probably more popular than Jesus. Just before the Fab Four's 1966 North American tour, Lennon's comments created an uproar. Previously he had speculated that "Christianity will go. It will vanish and shrink. . . . I don't know which will go first—rock and roll or Christianity," musings that drew the wrath of Bible Belt fundamentalists, who boycotted Beatles concerts and recordings. Still, Lennon's audience of teenagers (including us) did not seem to blink, though our parents were either horrified or mildly perplexed. And John, Paul, George, and Ringo had no problems filling the pews in their concerts or selling record numbers of albums. When John Lennon spoke, kids tended to pay attention. In the nineteenth century, Nietzsche had already declared that God was dead, but he had had little impact on the broad masses in North America.

In spite of all the changes we have lived through, our respondents still are willing to designate some kind of religious affiliation for themselves. As we said in Chapter Three, women's education has taught us to be flexible, pragmatic, and willing to bend. So it is with our religion. What we have found in the surveys are women like the social worker from Calgary, Canada, who was raised in a traditional Anglican family but now describes herself as a "nature-based Buddhist." We find a former Presbyterian who now calls herself simply a "Protestant." Once a Lutheran, another respondent says she is now a "Protestant/Buddhist etc." A Baptist is now "nondenominational." An Episcopalian is now just a "Christian." Sometimes we want to reserve a corner for ourselves in the religious parking lot, so one respondent has listed herself as "spirituality based, nondenominational," holding to the broadest-based criteria, while still reserving for herself the ability to take from this religious belief and that. In the Catholic church, a new genre of Catholics has been labeled "à la carte," which describes those who still call themselves Catholics; they dispute teachings on a number of issues while accepting others.

Daughters Value Their Mothers' Religious Teachings

Many daughters attribute their affiliation with religion and, more broadly, with a spirituality they treasure, to their mothers. Yes, mothers irritated us by making sure we went to temple or church, but some of it stuck. Actually, our religious training became transformed and continues as something we can choose to call on in a crisis or that quietly holds our ethical life together.

Ann's mother was a Methodist (her father, she says, had no religious affiliation), and now that she is thinking about it, Ann says what she discounted as a teenager she now values most: the "deep spiritual values my mother instilled in me. Mom always insisted we attend and participate in church. Either by coercion or threat, we were in church three times a week, and I hated it. Now that I'm grown, I am appreciative of the deep faith in God this childhood experience instilled. My faith and prayers have helped me through many rough patches in life. It's her greatest advice because it taught me to enjoy each day God gives you. Be a good example, as you may be the only Bible people ever read."

Sometimes we count ourselves as members of a faith but add layers to the spiritual search our mothers helped set us on. Cassie, the artist and former teacher from Alberta, now counts herself a churchgoing Catholic but says she is "also exploring a more personal spirituality and a greater understanding of a higher consciousness through a broad range of reading and through meditation."

We can (and frequently do) change our religion from that of our mothers, but that does not mean some essence of our mother's religious or spiritual teachings does not enrich our lives. Janis's mother, for example, was raised as a Catholic but married a divorced man, so was married "outside the church," as it is termed. She nevertheless decided to raise her five children in the Catholic faith. Now Janis has joined the Bahai religion and finds its religious tones quite in keeping with how her mother raised her. The Bahais have an eclectic view of religion, believing in the prophets from other religions: Moses, Jesus, and Mohammed. Their founder, the Persian Bahullah, said all religions honor the same God and preached that the highest form of worship is mutual acceptance of others.

Janis's mother was artistic, and eventually (after a stint in the WAVES, some social work, and work for the League of Women Voters) she turned to working in a fabric store and becoming an interior designer. She made a beautiful, comforting home, which Janis, in her turn, has also done. Growing up, "orderliness was next to godliness," she says. "This showed up in our having a physical environment that always looked beautiful depending on our means, and it gave me a real sense of security. Now my husband walks into our home, and I am in my sanctuary. He says, 'You've made this for me.'" The colors are blended, and it is a peaceful place, Janis says—an anchor that blends beyond her home to a larger sense of security and serenity: "This, I would say, I owe to my mother. She always brought beauty into our lives, and I think that that is a spiritual gift. Mom showed me that harmony, color, beauty, and orderliness bring peace of mind." Janis continues to seek that spiritual connection, outside her "sanctum" as well as inside. She belongs to a woman's group, "a kind of woman's spirit thing where we are in the process of self-discovery and searching and seeking spiritual answers, trying to make a meaning out of life, which includes making some kind of meaning out of yourself." From the home and hearth created by her mother, Janis has embarked on a road of spiritual discovery, which will stretch out in front of her for all of her life.

Some of us have followed the religious path our mothers suggested, but with some slight detours along the way. Bringing up the rear is fine with these women. Connie, a graduate student in history at the University of Cincinnati, remembers her parents' religion, which she once discounted and now embraces:

One of the things my mother always said was "believe that the Lord will provide." My parents were hard workers, and they didn't have a lot of things materially in life. They owned their own home in a working-class neighborhood. They had financial worries. Mom used to say she "robbed Peter to pay Paul." I thought they were naive to place so much trust in the Lord, always finding "a way" for them to escape their problems. But, by the age of forty-eight, after living in a pretty bad marriage that lasted twenty-six years, I turned to the Lord and said, "Okay, I don't know what's ahead, but my life is yours. You will get me through." Times aren't always easy, but I know that if I do the best I can, I am where God (or some kind of higher power) wants me to be and that for whatever reason this dilemma in my life is a growing experience.

This kind of basic belief in God's strength has played a more traditional role for some members of our respondent community. It ranges from "keeping the faith, making it important in your life" since it will come in handy during the rough patches, to a belief in prayer as a bedrock for our lives. Some women give prayer a power to change things. Others say the community of the church is an important ingredient in some baby boomer women's lives—the belief that there are others out there willing to stand beside you as a member of their religious community. Again, all this belief stems from their mother's example.

This more traditional faith has also been translated into a language we can use for the times we live in and the times we have lived through. Women who follow the traditional path are more likely to cite the belief in ethics, a broad spirituality, and the importance of honesty, all thanks to their mothers. Generally it bears just a slight resemblance to the catechisms and sermons we were taught as little girls. Now, though, it is less specific and with fewer rules to abide by. It is broader and diffuse. It frequently resonates around the idea that one must love oneself to be able to love anyone else and that love comes from the "deep heart's core," as the Irish poet Yeats called it. It is also frequently married to the idea that God (or whoever) wants us to reach out to others and to help the less fortunate, which has had an incredible impact as baby boomer women have sallied forth to work in the civil rights movement, the environmental movement, politics, and in aiding the less fortunate, subjects explored in Chapter Seven.

Sally, the special education administrator from Chicago, has been through what she calls "a disastrous first marriage" and admits to making a few mistakes along the way. The greatest strength her mother has passed along to her, she believes, "is my inner strength and a deep spiritual core that allows me to believe in myself and to love." From the mother's deep and more traditional beliefs in one God comes the daughter's larger, more generalized belief in a spirituality that embraces much. For Karen Guiterrez, a manager in the training and development division of Procter & Gamble, her spirituality is based on her mother's dedication to God: "I think my attitude that I am indebted to God for all he's done for me comes from my mom, but this is a positive for me because it motivates me to 'give back,' to work to better the conditions of others who may not have been as fortunate in certain ways." This is true, although her biggest arguments with her mother surround her mother's "absolutism" on abortion and the Catholic church's insistence on its infallibility. "For her, there's no middle ground, whereas I see more gray areas due to life's complexities," says Karen.

Do Unto Others

Respondents cited one consistent "rule" more than any other that their mothers impressed on them: the Golden Rule, or "do unto others," which respondents cite simply as thus: "Mother said, 'Always treat others like you want to be treated.' Never make fun of anyone because of their actions, words, or looks." Kathy, the computer instructor, hopes that she can pass on her mother's advice about The Golden Rule to her own daughter. She admires the way her mom "treated others with respect, patience, and love." It was certainly what the Beatles sang about, as in "all you need is love," a notion often discounted by the popular media now.

Respondents who disagree with their mother's views on intermarriage cite a religious belief in tolerance as their guiding light. Colette, the adjunct instructor in education from Chicago, says her mother, a Lutheran, cautioned her against getting involved with Catholic men "because I would be pregnant all the time and he would be in the bar with his buddies. It was the worst advice because it's so stupid! Prejudice based on very limited information caused me to question what could have turned into very valuable friendships and relationships."

As baby boomer women struggle to balance all the things competing for their attention, those who have found religion or spirituality important in their lives try to pass that on to their daughters. If Karen could choose one thing her mother passed to her and send that along to her daughter, it would be this: that although girls can do anything if they work hard enough, she "will need a sense of humility and an acknowledgment that we can't do it alone and need to look to God for help sometimes. I'd add a quote I heard once, which is, 'Pray as if everything depended on God, and act as if everything depended on you.'"

The Reverend Katherine Hancock Ragsdale

In June 1995, Reverend Ragsdale was invited to speak to a conference in Cincinnati on religious issues surrounding freedom of reproductive choice. Over three hundred people crowded the Westin Hotel's Ambassador Ballroom to hear her declare, in calm and assuring words, that the theology of many religions allows for the conscientious decision to terminate a pregnancy. Cincinnati was a fitting place for this message: it was there that the first firebombing of an abortion clinic took place in the United States (in 1978) and where the Right to Life movement was founded by Dr. Jack Willke. Ten years before Ragsdale spoke as president of the Washington-based Religious Coalition for Reproductive Choice, the historic landmark building owned by Planned Parenthood and called the Margaret Sanger Clinic had been destroyed by a firebomb. Here, too, a city council member who had proposed a city ordinance that would have mandated the burial of aborted fetuses rose in the political hierarchy to become Ohio's first black secretary of state. And prior to the reverend's arrival, a Hamilton County commissioner had sent a letter to the city's Methodist ministers telling them he thought their support for abortion was contrary to Methodist teachings. (The ministers objected to his views.) Ragsdale's speech also came shortly after the fatal shooting of two abortion clinic workers in Brookline, Massachusetts. It was a good time to preach calmness and clear-headedness when it came to religion and this difficult moral issue.

You might think that Reverend Ragsdale had been raised in a religious family, but she says that is not so. Her family attended an Episcopal church on a regular basis when she grew up in Newport News, Virginia. But it really was her mother's no-nonsense view of religion and how it needed to outfit its believers with strong, moral beliefs, minus the need for "God magic," that Katherine believes most influenced her view of religion and, thus, the career she has chosen and the life she leads. Now she is an Episcopal priest at St. David's Church in a small community north of Boston and recipient of a doctorate from the Episcopal Divinity School in June of 1997.

Katherine remembers a day when she was six or seven. Her family, including her mother, Ann, father, Coleman, younger brother, Edwin, and younger sister, Harriet, were driving home from church. Katherine's parents were engaged in a conversation about what they had just heard from the pulpit:

My mom said to my dad, "You can't just expect God to come in and fix things for you." I remember being appalled! I was at that age when God was supposed to be magic—what's the point of God otherwise? Of course, my mother wasn't talking to me but having this conversation with my father. My mother was someone who did care about the church, but she wasn't checking her brain at the door. She still remains practical, thoughtful, and questioning—not a bad model. But when I first heard that—that any worthwhile religion has to stand up to reality and serious questions—it was sort of a horrifying notion.

Ann Hancock Ragsdale had grown up on a farm in Beaver Dam, Virginia, forty-five minutes north of Richmond. She hated farm life and left for Richmond, where she met her future husband, who would spend his work life in retailing. Before she married Coleman, she became a secretary, traveled with her friends to the beaches of the Carolinas, and even visited Cuba. She attended the opera and the ballet. As a wife, she had to leave the traveling and the arts behind since the family moved frequently and had little money left over for frills. She had been voted the most likely to succeed in her high school class, but now, says Katherine, she was often unhappy "because she was underutilized. She was a bright, ambitious person with not many options." She was also a great reader, as was Katherine, and encouraged her daughter to ask questions about anything or read anything that was lying about and be interested in everything.

When Katherine enrolled in English and religion at the College of William and Mary, she was well prepared for a rigorous examination of world religions and her own faith:

I remember one of my professors saying, "Look, I don't want to get letters from your parents saying how I've made you lose your faith. If this course can make you lose your faith, then you never had it." The course was historical, critical biblical work, and I certainly saw people having a lot of struggles with that. Then, when I went to the Virginia Theological Seminary, those who hadn't done it in college were having a crisis: "If the Bible isn't literally true, then what's the nature of my faith?" That's never been a problem for me, and I hadn't made the connection until now with what I knew all the way growing up about my mother's faith. That is, you can question the accuracy of things in the Bible; you can question anything. And you can still feel perfectly faithful.

In the contemplative climate of the seminary, Katherine started reading works by feminist theologians and began to see that her mother's life, as well as her own, was shaped by the times they were born into. Her mother did not go to college or live the fuller life she could have wished for; equally, Katherine labored under what she remembers as a "very oppressive, male-oriented seminary." But now she sees the practicality and wisdom of her mother as a solid foundation for her theological studies and her career and the feminine stress on reaching out to others, showing courtesy and proper manners as "really, a way of making life more comfortable for everyone, showing respect for everyone."

Creative Daughters

The worlds of creativity and spirituality are not so distant from one another, as we saw in our respondents' surveys. As with Janis, whose relationship with her mother's Catholicism was described earlier in this chapter, the spiritual often feeds the creative, and vice versa. So often, as we contemplate God or our inner life, we use our reservoirs of creativity. As Shaun McNiff argues in his wonderful book, *Earth Angels: Engaging the Sacred in Everyday Things*, "There is always a sense of angels when we hear descriptions of how poems, paintings, and music emanate from the soul in the flying sparks of the creative spirit. The artist is the agent or 'active' instrument through which the soul expresses itself and realizes its purpose. This is why the creative arts are always wedded to religion and spirituality. The freer the artist's spirit, the more it expresses the divine energy." The poet Wallace Stevens was more succinct: "It is life that we are trying to get at in poetry. God and the imagination are one."

How do you light a creative fire under a squirming child who prefers to run outside and jump rope with her friends? How do you say to her that possibly, just possibly, she might not become the next Alicia de la Roca if she practices the piano, but she will learn to love music and the harmonies of life (bird sounds, far-off trains, whistling for us to follow them)? How do you make a little girl realize that although she looks delicious in her tutu, she is not likely to become Margot Fonteyn, but she should enjoy the dance for as long as she lives? Our mothers, often denied expensive music lessons or dance lessons or lessons in painting, tried to give us these "enhancements" in the 1950s and 1960s, often thinking it would be good for us, would teach us discipline, and would give us something else to enrich our lives. According to our respondents, this often was the case. But there was a proviso from mom: enjoy and learn from your experiences, but do not consider music, writing, acting, or anything similar as a good way to earn your living.

Some respondents think all those hours of structured after-school lessons were too much for their free spirits, as did Jenny, the wine wholesaler from Illinois. Her mother had her coming and going to piano, ballet, foreign language lessons, art appreciation classes, and various athletic pursuits. "I think that as a child, my mother kept me too busy. I was always having to have some extra interests, not giving me much time to just do nothing, like watch TV after school. This is still an issue for me over the last years, as I find it very difficult to just do nothing—sit and relax. But her thoughts were to give me experiences, and that I can appreciate." Most women in our survey, however, particularly those on the early end of the baby boom, are now thankful for the lessons they received in arpeggios and glissade.

Marjorie, the fitness consultant from Edmonton, said her creativity is linked with her mother's love of piano playing. Marjorie has played for friends' wedding receptions, family parties, and other places where she knows she will be well received. And there are no harsh reviews in the *Edmonton Journal* afterward. With her Yamaha baby grand piano, she can sit down and play for her own enjoyment as well.

In my case (VWR), my mother did the same for me. She was a good pianist who was (and still is) able to play some difficult Chopin pieces; she is a good sight reader and can play Christmas carols and, with her sister, Virginia, piano duets like "Marche Militaire." I studied piano too, practicing up to three hours a day before I quit. I have a wonderful grand piano just waiting for me to begin practicing my scales and Bach Inventions. Like Marjorie, whatever my skill level, I have a deep love of music—all kinds—that I can trace directly back to my mother and father. Standing around the piano and singing is a great joy to me, and one of the best times is when my mother is seated at the keyboard.

Gina, a dispatcher for a truck company in Springfield, Illinois, told us that of all the kinds of influence her mother had on her, she was most stronly influenced by her mother's creativity. Although her mother's career was in supervising child adoptions, she dabbled in oil painting, all the while encouraging her daughter to play the piano, write, and appreciate "art in any form." She read Robert Frost's poetry to her children and other stories and poetry—"quite sophisticated, like we were older kids," remembers Gina. The idea was to get her kids to develop good taste, their own ideas, and their own patterns for living. Now, Gina would rather spend her money on prints for her living room—such as Georgia O'Keeffe and Native American artist Oscar Howe—than on clothes. And she belongs to four book clubs as well as the Library of America.

Laurie, a secretary from Colorado, also singled out her mother's effect on her own creativity as her most powerful influence. Her mother, also an executive secretary, encouraged her four kids to play with creative toys (some she made herself). This mother encouraged "every poem I wrote, every picture I painted, anything I could dream up." Our mothers probably knew they did not have a future Georgia O'Keeffe on their hands. Their job was simply to encourage us to get our paint on the canvas and then praise the result, no matter how awful.

Creativity in the Kitchen—
In Spite of Home Economics

Some of us hated home economics and the numbing, cookie-cutter approach to the creative arts in the home: cooking, sewing, interior decorating. But some of us were lucky enough to have mothers who, as they tried to find a new way of stretching the family budget and disguising hamburger, taught us to love that same thing. Some women in our survey now proudly report that thanks to their moms, they know how to sew, crochet, and knit (when they have the time or sometimes as a tension reliever) and appreciate crafts. And cooking has now become an art form (when we have the time to indulge). Martha Stewart's publications and all the other home and garden magazines are the fastest-increasing segment of the magazine industry.

Our mothers may have felt that a well-chosen, appropriately cooked roast of beef with perhaps a tomato aspic was the crowning glory of a dinner party. Now we whomp up meals with elaborate dishes with regional flavors and ingredients from around the world. Mom made scalloped potatoes; now, *Bon Appétit* provides recipes for "scalloped potatoes with goat cheese and herbes de Provence." Maybe ice cream with chocolate sauce would do for mom's dinner party; now, *Bon Appetit* would recommend "frozen nougat terrine with bittersweet chocolate sauce and raspberry fig sauce." We use condiments and spices our mothers could not have bought at Safeway, even if they had wanted to. In a 1946 issue of *Ladies' Home Journal*, the "mouth-watering" menu featured and photographed in color (not all articles were given that honor) included rib roast of beef, mushroom consommé, Yorkshire pudding, lima beans, franconia potatoes, tomatoes, rolls, green salad, and upside-down cake. Now fast-forward to December 1996, and *Bon Appétit*'s version of red meat and the trimmings featured beef tenderloin with chipotle and cilantro sauces, roasted poblano tamales, fiesta shrimp with peppers, vegetables en escabeche, grapefruit and jicama salad, and cinnamon flan.

We found that our respondents—even Wandering Daughters—gave high marks to their mothers for reminding them that the household arts are important. Although Marilyn, an office manager from Cincinnati, blames her mother for many of her problems—she married at nineteen just to get out of the home—she still credits her mother with fostering her creativity. "My mother was from a very poor family of immigrants. She can sew and taught my Girl Scout class about sewing. I learned how to cook by watching her. She used to decorate cakes, and I watched her do that. She likes to use her hands. I'm very creative and probably got it from her."

There's No Business Like Show Business

Some daughters have used their mother's encouragement to pursue careers in the arts. Cassie, from Red Deer, Alberta, has become a painter and artist since leaving the teaching profession. Her husband is the chair of an arts department in the city's junior college, and their home is full of both their artwork (and that of other area artists they want to encourage). No longer obliged to grade papers and do lesson plans, Cassie has embarked on a business selling elaborate angels, St. Nicholas figures, and other dolls she and a friend design and create for gift shops. Neither of her parents was creative; she says "their attitudes were too practical to allow for that kind of risk taking; but I know and appreciate myself to be very creative. I don't push extreme boundaries, but I have a deep love of color and beauty, and this was recognized by my mother."

Sally Clark, a playwright and painter from Vancouver, British Columbia, has fashioned her career out of painting (portraits and landscapes), then playwriting, and now both. Her plays have often taken an ironic or comical (or both) look at women's lives now and in the past. And although her mother is not an artist (she competed at Wimbledon before marrying Sally's father, a lawyer from Canada), she made sure her daughter took drawing, painting, dance classes, and music lessons from an early age. Sally's mother thought acting and painting were selfish and that her daughter should pursue something in the helping professions (teaching, nursing), but she also thought writing and illustrating children's books were suitable for Sally.

Billie, an actress from Illinois, answered our questionnaire about her mother with great enthusiasm, giving her mom, a nurse, high marks for having encouraged her to take a chance on show business and acting. Given her mother's own lack of experience in this area, Billie finds her enthusiasm for such a career goal quite surprising but the best advice her mother could give her: "I just respect the fact that my mother encouraged my acting and was supportive. Even though I'm not a star or making tons of money, she said, 'Go for it.' With theater, it wasn't, 'No, you can't major in that.' She just let me find my own way, and even though it's been very difficult, I've done it all by myself. I just tease my mom and say that she was too good a mom."

Combining the helping and creative professions has proved a good middle ground for many daughters who honed their creative talents and then followed a more traditional role of teaching. That is the case for Sylvia, a music teacher in the public schools and a church music director. Although her mother's own occupation was as a telephone operator, Sylvia says her musical talent was nurtured from a very early age in modest but entirely successful ways by her mom: "Mom sang to us and with us as far back as I can remember. Oh, we'd harmonize while doing dishes or riding in the car. I've wanted to sing as long as I can remember. Mom and Dad paid for violin, piano, viola, and voice lessons for me. Mom did my chores so I could practice. While I was attending graduate school, Mom watched my children, paid my tuition, did my laundry, and attended my concerts. I have really been blessed!"

If we think that we could have been a contender in the arts but that our mothers did not encourage us or our mothers actively discouraged us, then they take the blame for our failures. Wendy, who has had a series of short-term jobs lasting two years or less, has tried her hand in technical or service-oriented fields and is currently job hunting. She blames her mother, a teacher, for discouraging her musical career: "Music is ultimately where I belong and is a joyous thing for me. But her lack of support for that pursuit discouraged me from what should have been the most important and best thing I could have done."

Pat Mora, Poet

Writers know how difficult it is to sift through all the ideas running through their heads, getting them down on paper (or now, on the computer screen), allowing this effort to sit, and then sending it off to their editor, then to the scrutiny of the reviewers, and finally, the toughest of all, to the inspection of their readers. Our creation can be lost amid the pile of other books and old magazines; dinner can be dropped on it; children can take their crayons and slash through our words. The younger we are, the more frightening this prospect of publishing can be, even to a narrow audience of family or teacher. The young especially need the wisdom and guidance of someone they trust, someone who is close to them.

. Pat Mora was lucky at the beginning of her writing career, for her mother was her editor and an equally enthusiastic lover of words. This was accomplished in two languages, English and Spanish, for Pat grew up in a Hispanic home in El Paso, Texas, where both languages were spoken and were in fact interchangeable; as a result, she writes and thinks equally in both languages, as did her mother. Like most other Hispanic women growing up in the 1950s and 1960s, school administrators actively discouraged children from speaking Spanish, so for years, many of Pat's classmates would not have known that she could speak Spanish. It was easier for her, a somewhat shy child, to keep silent about this.

Pat's mother, Estela Delgado, had also grown up in a bilingual world, strictly demarcated between home and school. In the El Paso schools, only English was spoken. At home, Estela's father insisted on Spanish and nothing else. "When you enter this house, Daughter, you are in Mexico," she remembers her mother telling her. Those being the ground rules, Estela became the family translator, handling "everything," says Pat. Estela even entered speech contests on the state level—in English. Although Estela became proficient in both languages, there was no money for her to go on to college. "She would tell me," says Pat, "'I don't know how I did it, those speech contests. My parents didn't know what I was saying; nobody could listen to my speech. I would just tell them that I'm going to the contest.'"

In spite of Estela's lack of formal education, she was Pat Mora's first, and best, editor. She read everything Pat wrote and would critique it, helping Pat rework awkward phrases. She has saved the small essays, early efforts, and everything else that Pat has published or written, which is considerable. Mora is the author of fifteen books of poetry, nonfiction, and children's books. She writes in both languages, and her work has found its way into collected volumes such as *The Best American Poetry of 1996*. Pat credits her success to the gentle nurturing of her mother:

> From the time I started writing, I always took my papers to Mom to see what suggestions she'd make. She'd carefully read what I wrote, pick up her pen, and in what I thought was such beautiful penmanship, begin to propose ways I might improve what I'd written. Her suggestions were gentle and helpful. I would also practice any

speeches I gave with her, her suggestions a kind of safety for me. I enjoyed speaking before the class or school from the time I was in grade school, just as Mother had. She gave me a deep love of words, and I really value the fact that she's bilingually articulate as a writer. We both really love words, you know, and I would say that's even beyond just liking books. We both really like putting words together. She's very good at that, and so, when she looked at a paper, I could always count on her to improve it. And really, she felt pride in her children. She would just let you know, "I am Pat's mom. I'm Mrs. Mora, and I taught her all she knows, and I am very proud."

The gentle humor that infects much of what Pat Mora writes comes directly from her mother as well. Pat sees this gift from her mother as a natural outgrowth of her love of words.

Thanks to her strong mother, Pat is a great defender of her culture. "Let's face it," she says, "the reality of the border is that there is a good culture, and then there is an inferior culture. Whether you want to or not, you are spending part of your life proving that you can do this other thing well. Certainly my way was eased by the fact that I had a mother who was extremely comfortable in this other world. And so I was able to go back and forth between the two."

But always, with women who made it and who look back at the mother waving them on (showing their first published poetry to friends and relatives), there is a sadness that their mothers, equally deserving, did not have the chances they did and did not have the kind of mentor in their own mothers that they were able to provide their daughters. Estela's parents were immigrants who came to the United States at the time of the Mexican Revolution. Pat's mother had to take jobs in department stores to help with the family finances. And when she married at age twenty-three, she stepped into a traditional setting where her husband ran his optical business and she was busy raising her four children. Her mother, Amelia, and sister, Ygnacia, also lived with them, so "she would clean all day long," says Pat. This lack of a creative outlet and the constant need to be a mother led to Estela's great unhappiness, and eventually she consulted a psychiatrist. The psychiatrist told her she needed a creative outlet, so her husband bought her a piano. Once she had taken lessons and had loved to sing, so perhaps this would bore a hole through the wall of the family and give Estela her chance. It all helped some, says Pat, but still, there could have been more:

> I would say the piece that I am missing with my mother is that I don't have a full sense of what she suffered. I think that's always the hard piece. I can guess it was hard growing up—this for a little girl who was so bright and who made it on her own, but I think this must have been really hard—hard not to go to college, hard to be in a marriage where she didn't develop parts of herself. But she will say, "Well, you know if I go [die] now, it's perfect. I have seen all of my children. I have never lost a child. I have never lost a grandchild, and I have never been really ill." And I say to her, "I understand, I understand."

7

Manners Don't Cost Money

I first realized I was like my mom when I was in my thirties. I remember reaching out to help a relative stranger and thinking, "This is what my mom would be doing."
Gillian, forty-year-old school administrator, San Francisco

Mother's admonitions began simply, even innocuously: "Mind your manners"; "People of good breeding don't do that"; "Kill 'em with kindness"; "If you can't say something nice, don't say anything at all" (this cliché was the most frequently cited by respondents, as told to them by their moms); "Look after your little brother [or sister]"; "Don't stare at people who are different from you"; "Go visit your grandparents"; "Don't forget to send Aunt Anne a birthday card, and remember to buy a shower gift for your cousin Marilyn [the one we couldn't stand]"; "You'll have to go to Sheldon's bar mitzvah even if you think he's a jerk. His parents are our friends and they'd be hurt." And "Remember the Girl Guides' [or Girl Scouts'] motto: On my honor, I promise to do my best, . . . to help other people every day and to obey the Guides' Law."

From these simple words of admonition from our mothers, baby boomer women began to understand that we were being prepared for a role in the larger world, where manners and getting along and caring are vital for success. Our moms could not imagine that we would play such a pivotal role in social change. For example, the estimable United Way of America found Elaine Chou to take over the helm in 1992, making her the first woman to run that powerful agency. Nor could our mothers foresee how we would begin to inch our way into the political world, as did Geraldine Ferraro, who was Walter Mondale's running mate in the 1984 presidential election. In Canada, boomer Kim Campbell was elected Canada's first female prime minister in 1993, where her record as a cabinet minister was dissected in minute detail compared with that of her opponent, Jean Charet.

Like a small stone dropped into a still pond, with the radiating, concentric circles of our interest outside ourselves—to our next of kin, our friends, our neighbors, our coworkers, and the larger world where social injustice needed changing—our mothers' constant urgings to do the right thing have made an enormous difference in our lives.

Starting with the Basics

Where did these future directors of social agencies, mayors, senators and congresswomen, CEOs of environmental agencies, and town officials come from? If they were women, they came from environments created by their mothers where the basics of caring for others were stressed. From them we learned that thinking of someone other than ourselves—as opposed to our brothers, who often were told to make their way to the head of the class by outwitting everyone else or by scoring very high on their SATs—was the secret of success.

Some of us were headstrong and needed constant reminding about the importance of caring for others, remembering their feelings, and subduing our instincts to say what we *really* thought. For Jeannelle, the airline engineer, her social worker mother's constant teachings on the subject of "do unto others" were very annoying. She remembers that her mom used to say she "didn't give enough consideration to the feelings of others. I figured people should have thicker skins. What did feelings have to do with anything? Now I know what she said was true, and I cringe at some of the things I said when I was younger. Today I'm very conscious of the feelings of others, and I'm a better person because of it."

Michelle, one of the women we got to know in a meeting with a group of respondents from Cincinnati, would seem the very embodiment of a well-behaved and polite woman. A graduate student in history at the age of fifty, she is now coming to appreciate her mother's nagging about the importance of being a well-brought-up young lady:

> I used to hate it when my mom would say, "There are things in life you'll have to do you won't want to do." Now, I was bent and determined that no one could make me do what I didn't want to do. I was a very dutiful child, but when I got a little older, I'd rebel against this rule of mom's on a small scale—maybe not attend a distant relative's funeral though the whole family went. I truly believed I could go through my life for the most part doing only pleasant things that I chose to do. My attitude was that she and Dad were *nuts* doing things for others and putting themselves out when they could have been doing pleasurable things for themselves. But over the years I've come to understand that these tough things in life we're called on to do challenge us to live our lives as active participants through all the experiences life has to offer.

This is a sentiment that Kathy, a computer instructor from Minnesota, agrees with. Reflecting on advice her mother offered that she thought was quite useless at the time, she now believes that her mother's emphasis on manners—things like thank-you notes, proper greetings and good-byes, and general etiquette—was essential in her development: "In my younger years, I did what I was told but grumbled underneath. Now, as an adult, I can see the whole world is a better place because of our consideration for others."

Learning About Friendship

While the process of learning to take other people's feelings into account was working its alchemy on our respondents, they also credit their moms with teaching them about friendship and the creative, dynamic, and important part that our friends would play in our lives. It was true for some of us that when we got to be teenagers and a certain someone did ask us out, we would scrub plans we had made with our best friend to spend that evening going to the movies with her for a date with what's-his-name. Funny thing, though: he has now likely gone the way of all flesh, but she may still be important to us. If not, her friendship as we were growing up provided a kind of laboratory where we experimented with the give and take necessary in any relationship and the flexibility so important in our work life.

"My mom taught me to take an interest in who people are and to look deep and make my relationships meaningful, to care for my friends, be there for them, and not be obsessed with my own self," says Kathy. Or, as Rhonda, a nurse, tells it, her mother taught her to be "caring and sensitive about others' feelings and to be helpful, lend an ear when needed, and to be there for a friend."

Friendship did not have to be with those who were just like ourselves, say respondents. "My mother has had a couple of long-enduring relationships with other women, neither of whom is much like her," says Alice, the self-employed medical transcription specialist from California. "I've learned to value differences and learned to be tolerant and to see what I can learn from other women who are unlike myself."

A minority of respondents think their mothers were too wrapped up in their own family worries; still, the majority believe their mothers' social skills reached beyond that narrow sphere. Most of our mothers' friendships understandably would have been with other women (friendships with the opposite sex were less socially acceptable then than they are now). This has meant that women respondents cite their friendships with other women as a deep and abiding gift from their mothers that will take them a long way through this life. Sophie, the professional fundraiser from Ohio, says:

> My best friends are women and always have been. This can only be attributed to my mother's influence. Even as a teenager, she emphasized that friendships with girls were more important than relationships with boys. "Your girlfriends will be there after your boyfriends are long gone," she used to say. Or, as I got older, "Women have it tough enough in this world without making it tougher for each other." Women have to stick together. My mom and her friends used to look as if they were having such fun! I looked forward to growing up and doing the same things my mom and her friends did: shopping, antiquing, taking painting classes together, drinking tea. And laughing!

Responsibility to Our Fellow Creatures

As the circle reaches out to its farthest point, we find this generation of baby boomer women intensely interested and involved in social issues, again, thanks in large part to mothers.

Annie, the aerobics instructor who once suffered from scoliosis, thanks her mother for making it clear that her best self would recognize the need to stand up for herself and for others: "Mom taught me to have empathy and compassion for others, to reach out to those who are not as happy or as fortunate. I was told that everyone had sadness, problems, and other issues that made them less fortunate." When she was down, her mother would remind her that "you're not the only person who is sad—everyone has sadness and problems. You just don't see them."

"Eat everything on your plate—think of the starving Chinese," our mothers would drill into us. Or, as one respondent said, her mother urged her kids to be grateful they had something to eat; the "starving Armenians would like to have what we had," she reports her mom urging as her children looked gloomily at unwanted helpings of stew. Later in life, "starving Armenians" and all that this connoted made this respondent "aware of the need for social justice in the world." Again and again, women in the survey note, sometimes with surprise, the gift of compassion their mothers gave them. Karen Guiterrez, a brand manager at Procter & Gamble, thanks her mother for this gift, despite their differences when she was growing up: "My mother has been an extremely positive influence in my life. Her values of compassion, loyalty, and hard work, coupled with her visionary thinking, creativity, and enthusiasm, have been an inspiration to me. They have caused me to stretch myself to contribute as much as I can to the community and to my family." Her mom tended to turn their suburban Minneapolis home into a shelter for homeless people who might be living in a car, for example. "Every time I came home from college, there'd be new people in the house," Karen recalls.

Karen's mom, Marj, took her Catholicism as a call to help others and spent two Christmases volunteering in war-torn Bosnia. Her daughter is no slouch herself. She helped found an enormously successful mentoring program in the Cincinnati public schools, pairing fifteen hundred kids and fifteen hundred adults in an experiment that is now permanently funded and supported by the city's elite business leaders. She is a leader with Women Helping Women in Cincinnati, an organization that assists women who have been raped or stalked or are the victims of domestic violence or incest, and she has been asked to help teach police rookies how to deal with these crimes. In spite of having two small children (and a husband) and a full-time job, she was named a Kellogg Fellow with a $100,000 grant to develop her leadership role. She travels the globe, does research, develops a plan, and has begun a program to cope with teenage sexual activity. It is a straight line from mother to daughter.

Karen Kain, Prima Ballerina, National Ballet of Canada

Watching prima ballerina Karen Kain pirouette across the stage and through her life as one of Canada's most important dancers, as partner to the late Rudolf Nureyev, and as interpreter of choreographer Roland Petit's balletic version of *Carmen*, the first thought that comes to mind is not necessarily that her mother's greatest gift to her was empathy, but it was. Kain remembers her mother as tremendously thoughtful of others, but she also enjoyed all sorts of people and would happily wade into a crowd in any situation.

Yet as she considers her mother's impact on her life, soon after Winnifred's death from liver cancer in the summer of 1996, Karen believes this empathy has played a great role in her own life and in the dance world. Of course, thinking about another dancer in the corps de ballet who may be getting the ax is not the optimal way to concentrate on one's performance. It could be distracting sometimes, when Karen instead needed to be thinking clearly about her performance. Nonetheless, this gift has had a tangible and important impact on the dance world. Karen has served on the board of the Dancer Transition Resource Center in Toronto, which trains dancers for careers beyond the stage, something few dancers are prepared for. Dancers donate portions of their salary to the organization, which is matched by their dance companies. The money is there to train dancers for careers elsewhere. Kain says some have become doctors, vets, chefs, physiotherapists. That is what she remembers her mother being right about—"looking after people and being generous to other people"—much of which Winnifred had shown Karen by example.

The stereotype of the self-obsessed prima ballerina is not the kind of girl Winnifred raised. Kain empathized with her fellow dancers all along the way: "I'd see other dancers I knew were not going to make it as a classical dancer. I saw people fall by the wayside. It was a heartbreaker." Seated in her armchair in her historic landmark home in North York, Ontario, Karen Kain, beautiful at forty-five, even without makeup, assesses the differences between her mother and herself and things that her mother was right about, particularly the importance of "looking after people and being generous to other people. Now I go, 'oh yes, she was right about that.' It was more in her example of being with people."

Not Quite the Mom of *Ladies' Home Journal?*

As we compiled the results of our survey, the picture of our mothers looked much more complicated. Although few mothers became civic leaders (though some did) in the same way our fathers might have, they did play a role in their communities by their volunteer work and their insistence that their daughters owed something more to society than nabbing a decent fiancé. "I decided that I had similarities close to my mom when I was in my teens," says one respondent. "I was fighting for what I believed in, breaking ground as a girl in a boys' world. I felt proud and scared and angry at the forces in place—but determined to succeed despite them." Sometimes we recognize these similarities with a sudden jolt, as with one respondent who remembers that her civic duty came from her mother: "It was in my forties when I felt I had similarities close to my mother. I was with her and was telling her about contesting a traffic ticket and writing letters to the mayor and city attorney. I felt independent and able to communicate."

For Linda, the magazine production manager from Vancouver, her mother's social consciousness is quite amazing in retrospect: "She had an incredible sense of civic duty. After bearing two children, my sister and myself, my parents decided to adopt a third child of mixed race. He has turned out to be emotionally unstable, schizophrenic, and probably suffers from fetal alcohol syndrome. But I think that they think they've done the right thing."

As mom directed our energies to the world outside our living room window, she reminded us that we needed to be sure "to help those less well off and to care for anyone or anything that needed help, i.e., the elderly, less fortunate people, animals," a respondent wrote.

A minority of respondents wonder at their mothers' motivation in always being "nice" or considerate to others to look good to everyone else, but by seeing this flaw in the formula, have themselves tried to "do the right thing" for the right reasons. Colette, whose mother warned her against Catholic men, recalls that her mother was "always there for other people," though Colette wonders if her mother might not have had a hidden agenda at times. Still, Colette acknowledges a "very strong value to reach out to others only when it honestly comes from the heart, never because I want something in return. This is also the only way I can accept help from others. Being true to this value has enabled me to help many, many people in various ways and to feel satisfaction from the helping." Colette has been an academic program adviser at a university in Denver and continues to teach at night.

Like Colette, a few respondents cite their mothers' racial or religious prejudices as something they have tried to overcome in their own lives. They remember this intolerance tempered by their mom's admonitions to be polite, kind, and considerate to others. Clearly, for our respondents, one value won out over the other.

The issue of how much to sacrifice—to family, friends, and others—is something boomer daughters are of two minds about. On the one hand, they saw their mothers giving and giving and for what, in the end? Says Greta, the teacher from Chicago, "I had a hard time understanding how she could give so much of herself and not demand more for herself. When I was younger, it looked to me like she received very little in return for her sacrifices. Was she right? I still don't know, as my life took a very different direction." Greta's mother worked at various blue-collar jobs as she raised five children.

It is possible that our mothers, all the while teaching us to love our neighbors as we loved ourselves, did not leave enough time for their own development. They may have expected their own needs to be met along the way as they sacrificed, and when this did not happen, the inequity of what they were doing fueled their resentments. We as their daughters have clearly embraced the need to help others, including those outside the family unit, but we also want space for our own development, leaving us with more expectations and less time in which to accomplish them.

You'll Go Further with Honey Than with Vinegar

As it happened, we needed these social skills as much as the education mom insisted on for our careers. Women have learned to understand simple or complex work organizations often based on the people involved—their distinct personalities, their likes and dislikes. Maureen Kempston Darkes, president of General Motors of Canada, frequently spends time on the production floor talking with her workers ("I'd be in trouble if I weren't in touch," she says). Women like Kempston Darkes understand that the person occupying the job has a life outside the workplace. In fact, women often reach out and above (or below) to network with other people to get the job done, all the time remembering their mother as saying, "Manners don't cost money so you should have good ones." Who remembers to buy the card for the coworker's birthday or organize the shower for the mother-to-be? More often than not, it is women in the workplace.

This nexus of trying to be both successful and considerate to coworkers is tightly woven for respondents. According to Antonia, a senior account executive in a marketing research firm, her mother's influence can be felt most strongly in how her career has developed: "Mom was always giving of herself and her time, and she didn't do something that she didn't belong to, by holding an office, for example. And I'm that way now: very giving of myself and my time. I'm always striving for a part of the management of the organization." While Antonia has done well in her career, she also volunteers, as does her mother.

For Gloria, a teacher in Indiana, her mother's advice—"Be nice to everyone and friendly and don't know a stranger"—was the most important thing her mom could have told her because, as she reflects, "my outgoingness and personality have brought me far in life. I feel that I am well respected and well liked." Janice, an international banker, a volunteer, and a mother herself, thinks she discounted her mother's advice when she was young "for constantly emphasizing the importance of making a good impression on people." In hindsight, she believes that it is critical because "you never know when that person may show up in an important position. Although this advice is a bit cynical and manipulative, I do think it's accurate. I get a bit sad to see that her assessment of the world may be truer than I care to admit."

From Etiquette to Activism

While it is true that American women and, to a lesser extent, Canadian women have not been elected to political office in the same numbers as their counterparts in Scandinavia or even Australia, there are more female governors and federally elected officials than our mothers could dream of. In Quebec, where dancer Margie Gillis lives, women did not get the right to vote in provincial elections until 1940 (though the federal government granted them the right to vote in federal elections in 1918 after women's stellar service in the armed forces and at home). Women who now occupy these important political leadership slots, like Cleveland political leader Jane Campbell, trace their grounding directly to their mothers who, though they were unlikely to run for office, showed their daughters the way.

Jane Campbell, Ohio County Commissioner

Jane Campbell is the kind of politician her mother would have expected her to be. Joan Campbell surrounded Jane with people in the anti–Vietnam War community, politicians, students, and volunteers for homeless shelters, not the usual fare for most young girls her age. Now Jane is one of three county commissioners of Cuyahoga County in northern Ohio, a county comprising a million and a half people in Cleveland and its suburbs.

No one should be surprised at what Campbell has achieved in the world of politics, least of all her mother. Dr. Joan Campbell, general secretary of the National Council of Churches in New York, always impressed on her daughter the importance of "investing in the community" and of giving something back to the place she came from.

The home Jane Campbell grew up in the 1950s and 1960s sounds like something out of a television series. Her dad was an attorney; her mother was deeply involved in church work and political campaigns. When they were young, Jane and her two brothers were told stories about how their grandmother grew up in a house that had been a stop on the Underground Railroad in southern Ohio, and other fascinating stories about the fight for justice. During the Vietnam War, Dr. Benjamin Spock came to the Campbells' home for a fundraiser, as did William Kunstler, attorney and author of *And Justice for All.* Students from the local Jesuit University boarded with the Campbell family and, in exchange, provided free babysitting. Mrs. Campbell saw early on that too many people in Cleveland were running out of resources (food, housing) so she decided to organize a food pantry at her church, which turned out to be the first Hunger Center in the city. Everyone knew the Campbells were a soft touch, according to Jane, so people would call their home when no one was available at the church to help. "I remember it being Christmas Eve and taking calls from people who were panicked because they didn't have any money," says Campbell. "It was Christmas, and there was my mother, piling us in the car, running out and shopping and taking the food to them. It wasn't so much what my mother said; it was what she did."

The Campbells' social net was not confined to politics or family. They had (and still retain) a large network of friends whom they would entertain at their large home. Her parents thus taught Jane the importance of making friends and maintaining those connections:

> My mother always had close friends, men and women. And my parents had close friends who were couples. There was a whole group around the church, four or five couples, raising their kids, sharing a lot of stuff, and these people I still know today. Some of them have given me money in my political campaigns; some of them are totally Republicans. But that didn't matter, because I was like part of the family. Every time we had a holiday, there were always some extra people at the table.

Now a mother of two children herself, Jane has married her political, social, and domestic concerns so that when she served on committees in the Ohio legislature, they usually revolved around aging and housing, children and youth, abused and neglected kids, Ohio schools, adolescent sexuality and pregnancy, and all the other issues that a mother-cum-politician might be expected to care about.

As one of Ms. magazine's "Eight Women to Watch in the 80s" and Good Housekeeping's "100 Young Women of Promise," Campbell will likely travel far beyond Cleveland in her political career. Yet she will always take with her her mother's example, advice, and emphasis on caring for others as well as herself:

> I think my mother's a combination of masculine and feminine qualities. She's got leadership and good presence and style and those sorts of things, but also she's an

extremely inclusive person, and she thinks about people's emotions. You know, sometimes men think other people exist in a kind of vacuum and they don't have a life. She always knows something intimate about everybody she deals with, sort of a remarkable situation. We tease her about being "Mother Confessor." She's got all kinds of people coming to tell her all kinds of wholly personal matters, partly because she's a pastor. But there are a lot of male pastors that this doesn't happen to. It's because she's a woman.

Terri Crisp, Animal Rights Activist

If Jane Campbell's mother lit a neon sign for her to follow, then Terri Crisp's mother did something more modest, but very much like many of the mothers in our survey. She planted small seeds in her daughter's early years—the kind that grew in fertile soil and then blossomed abundantly, so that both mother and daughter are a bit surprised at what Terri Crisp has become.

Terri's parents gave her a lot of latitude, and, as a result, she says she kind of flipped and flopped all over the academic map. She changed majors several times and still is a few credits short of a degree. Her mother, Virginia, was a housewife, though she did some teaching when Terri and her brother, Todd, were growing up in southern California. Terri's dad was a sales manager for Seven Up.

Terri Crisp has become one of North America's leading animal rights advocates and directs all emergency animal rescue services for United Animal Nations. She has been profiled by NBC News, named "Person of the Week" by ABC News, and written up in *National Geographic*. Beginning in 1983 during the floods in Alviso, California, through Hurricane Andrew in Florida, and then the incredible devastation of the Exxon *Valdez* oil spill, Terri has focused the attention of Americans and worldwide organizations on the humane treatment of animals and on the need to plan for and take care of them as well as humans during disasters.

There were always animals in the Crisp household and a caring environment established from the beginning. And Virginia, Terri's mother, a quiet, soft-spoken woman, always reminded Terri of the Golden Rule: to be kind to others (human and animals), to be thoughtful and respectful of what she saw around her. "I don't think that I could ever remember a time in my life when she has yelled or gotten cross with a person," says Terri. "She is such a kind and thoughtful person who values her friends very much." Terri values this trait in herself and has learned how important it is in volunteer work done under extremely stressful situations. "I'm very sensitive to people's feelings. Part of why I have been so successful in coordinating volunteers is that I can be very sympathetic to what their needs are while trying to balance the job itself. I don't lose sight of those individuals, and I am trying always to give them opportunities in each disaster to grow as individuals also."

Virginia inadvertently taught Terri independence and discipline. When Terri was twelve, her mother was diagnosed with tuberculosis and was sent to a sanitarium. Terri and her younger brother were not allowed to see their mother for over a year. When she was first in the county hospital, absolutely no contact could be made: "It was like she went to prison. She was like a murderer who had been put on death row, and no one had contact with her. My dad couldn't even visit her at that stage," says Terri. When Virginia was moved to another location, she and Terri could at least talk by telephone—something they do well at today, Terri laughs. It was a sad time for Terri when Virginia was gone. Young Terri was placed in charge of meals and housekeeping, after her grandmother had to go back to her own responsibilities: "After school, I would have to come home and do my homework, start dinner, do the dishes, do laundry, keep an eye on my brother. I didn't play and I couldn't play and I had no time to play. I remember standing at the sink, doing dishes and making dinner, while watching the neighborhood kids out playing, and I wanted to do that and I was angry that I couldn't. But it taught me discipline." Sometimes Terri would call her mother crying, wondering why she could not have money to buy a new dress to go to the school dance. Virginia would send her magazine articles about how to have a girls' night at home and make herself beautiful (facials, manicures, hair styles), just trying to buck her daughter up.

Thus, the combination of her mother's standards of caring for others and her own love of animals, plus a good dose of independence, have helped form Terri Crisp, animal rescue heroine. Sometimes she thinks (like so many other daughters in our survey) that her mother would have loved to do something like this, but the times in which our mothers reached maturity did not encourage such risk taking. "I always think that there is this part of my mom who sometimes wishes that she would get this wild hair and just go do something crazy," says Terri. "But to a degree, my mom, through me, is living out some of the things that she may have wanted to do in her life."

Compliment Others
When You Have the Chance

It is clear that the manners our mothers taught us have done much to enrich our lives emotionally and socially. Almost without exception, the need for kindness, for saying to someone (even if we're not absolutely sincere) that we admire their new earrings or what an adorable child they have raised, is a gift that baby boomer women in our survey credit to their mothers. Although we pride ourselves on being more open than our mothers' generation, and much more willing to discuss anything for the sake of honesty, we have come to understand that it isn't always necessary to say exactly what we want to say and that manners and tact are quite valuable.

Our respondents' written and spoken comments on this gift of manners and what it led to are usually in the form of surprise or wry humor—that these useless, "feminine" embroideries turned out to be critical in their lives now. And as a bonus, they have helped them understand the power and importance of social awareness and have enriched their careers in ways they'd never imagined. As with education, this is a gift whose formula has had a much different impact in our lives than our mothers had in mind as they reminded us to thank Grandma for that perfectly geeky dress she had given us for Christmas.

Finally, manners and social graces, our respondents reminded us, included learning the need to be a good listener. As one respondent said, "My mother's favorite cliché was, 'People love to talk about themselves, so listen and learn,' another critical skill in relationships and career building."

These ramifications created by mother's lessons on manners also mean that the baby boom generation needs to hand down something like this to our daughters. As Diana, the director of a social service agency in Cincinnati sees it, her mother's stress on social responsibility meant there's a "level of responsibility to the community to give back." But it doesn't stop there, says Diana. Her mother also reminded Diana and her sister, "Never forget: your children have to be shown that soon it will be their turn to make a difference in society."

Part III

A Bittersweet Harvest

An Apple Doesn't Fall Far from the Tree

*I was thinking of marrying this man who said, "I hope
you don't ever become like your mother." And I
suddenly realized that I was a lot like my mother.
So I said, "Well, you better leave now because I'll
probably be exactly like her."*

> Sally Clark, forty-three-year-old
> single playwright from Canada

Baby boomer women made a mission out of being different from
their mothers. Scoffing at the self-sacrificing lifestyles they led,
striving for our own self-fulfillment, working toward greater economic independence, defying the limitations that kept our mothers corralled into very circumscribed existences became our raison
d'être.

And so when that very first awareness, that split second of an
instant when we look in the mirror and see her smile, or when we
hear her words with the very same intonation escape from our lips,
we are shocked. How can this be? We shake our heads vehemently,
hoping whatever "mother similarity" we noticed would break loose
and fly away, or we slap ourselves as a way to make sure we do not
ever do or say that "mother thing" again.

Whether we like it or not, we not only share our mothers' genes,
but we are also greatly influenced by them as our earliest and most

potent role models (just as they were by their mothers). We cannot escape the influence of nature and nurture when it comes to our moms.

One of the survey questions asked respondents to describe the memory they had of their first realization that they had traits or qualities similar to those of their moms. Most of them report they were in their twenties when this resemblance lurched out from some corner of their memory bank. Some reacted to the discovery as though it were a long-lost treasure, feeling great joy, as did this fifty-year-old single teacher from Ohio who says, "I was at a social gathering, chatting and feeling perfectly at ease, and I thought, 'Oh, this is what they mean when they say that mother never knows a stranger.' I was elated when I realized that I had this same trait." A thirty-seven-year-old financial analyst, who is a married mother of two from California, was twenty-five, and her husband had a drug problem. She remembers thinking, "He can't do this to me. My mom wouldn't—and didn't—tolerate this, so I won't either. I felt empowered!"

For others, the discovery leaves them entangled, if just for an instant, in an emotional web of anger and shame. Elise, the thirty-five-year-old physical therapist assistant and a married mother of two from California, was in her thirties when, she recalls, "My husband and I were arguing (I can't remember about what), but I realized that I was acting like my mother (childish) and sounding like my mother (selfish or really self-centered) and it made me sick, embarrassed, and ashamed because I never thought I was like her. I don't want to be like her negative attributes."

And then there are others whose reactions are somewhat benign. Ellie, the forty-two-year-old married culinary consultant from Illinois, said that her husband "tripped over my mother's shoes while visiting her home. He laughed and stated to me, 'Now I know why you leave your shoes around. You're just like your mother.' I realized then that many of my quirks were just like Mom's. This awareness made me feel that although I never wanted to be like Mom, I'm truly very much like her, and that was okay."

Wandering Daughters tend to experience more torment over this discovery than do the Untraveled or Prodigals, especially since they are so zealous in patterning themselves in reverse of their moms. The angers and resentments that characterize their relationships tend to cast a sizable blind spot on anything positive about their moms' personal qualities. This discovery can catapult them even further away from being anything like their mothers, often to a place of pain and suffering—much like a Wandering Daughter I (BMc) worked with who sought counseling because she was experiencing significant depression along with numerous physical complaints. She was being verbally abused by both her husband and son. At one point in our therapy, I asked her why she did not just stand up for herself and tell her husband and son to go to hell. She looked at me in utter disbelief: "Why I could never do that!" When I asked why not, she said, "Because that's what my mother would do. She was always angry, screaming and yelling. And, I'm proud to say, I'm *nothing* like her." Her chest swelled with pride at this proclamation. Although she had worked hard at being nothing like her mother, the price she was paying in physical and emotional symptoms was hardly worth it. In therapy we focused on ways she could find a middle ground, somewhere between her mother's aggressive style and her passive one.

You Are Just Like Your Mother

For many of our respondents, husbands were a major harbinger of the news that we are like our mothers. Interestingly enough, these announcements have usually been made to punctuate a point in their favor. Carol Ann, the forty-nine-year-old teacher's aide and married mother of two, says she was in her forties when she had her realization: "I was with my husband and two children, and I must've said something to the children. My husband said, 'You sound just like your mother.' I wasn't happy with the comment because I thought she interfered too much and was too concerned with things that were none of her business."

Some husbands use the similarities as extra ammunition when trying to make a point or win an argument, as was the case with Jean, the thirty-nine-year-old homemaker and mother of two from Illinois whose mom suffers from lupus: "I was in my twenties. I was depressed and lying on my couch watching TV doing a crossword puzzle. My ex-husband found a picture of my mom in the same position and showed it to me. I was mortified."

The lowest blow is to be called by her name. A fifty-year-old property manager and married mother of one from Ohio was in her forties when her husband would comment that she was making the same statements as her mother to her son: "Then he would call me my mother's name, which infuriated me. What hurt me the most is that deep down inside, I knew that what he was saying was the truth." Being told we are like our mothers scores a couple of points for our husbands in a marital conflict, but being called by her name, well, that is a home run.

Our husbands can use our mothers as a weapon only if we do not happen to value the characteristic we are said to share with our mom. Cheryl Marie, a forty-two-year-old administrative assistant from Colorado, says, "I was in my late twenties or early thirties. I realized we had similar traits during my second marriage when I was learning to garden and when I started being more organized about work, grocery shopping, planning things, and so on. My second husband yelled at me during an argument and told me how 'perfect' I was, 'Just like your mother,' he said. I knew then I was a lot like her, and it was all the good things!"

You Sound Just Like Grandma

The ghosts of our mothers are resurrected most frequently while we are parenting her grandchildren. We are often flung into a time warp, back to our own childhood. For many of our respondents, this is the most shocking and disturbing of discoveries. Jennifer, mother of one from Illinois, says, "When I had my own child, I caught myself almost saying and doing some of the things she had said and done to me as a child. I was horrified at how ingrained they were and how an abusive and negative comment could come so easily to my lips when my child acted as I had at the same age." Appendix B summarizes our moms' most repeated sayings on child rearing.

The slightest hint of any similarity between them and their moms has Wandering Daughters reeling with a mix of intense emotions. Suzi, a thirty-nine-year-old secretary and married mother of one, says, "I was in my thirties when I realized I had some of her in me. It was when I was fighting with my own teenage son. I had to stop and tell him that if I ever acted like his grandmother again, he had my permission to slap the *#*#** out of me."

Prodigal Daughters can also be disturbed by these ghosts. Colette, a married mother of four from Illinois, had a similar experience when she said to one of her children, "'Who do you think you are?' This was my mother's favorite put-down phrase as I was growing up. As soon as I said it, I wanted to slap myself."

No matter how much we promise ourselves we will not be like her, especially when it comes to parenting, the powers of role modeling squelch the vow. Consider this from a forty-eight-year-old homemaker and mother of one from Illinois: "I was trying to get my young daughter to finish her meal and heard myself shouting my mother's words. I felt shocked and ashamed. I knew it was wrong, but it came out." Nevertheless, we can use these moments to teach ourselves how not to be like her, thereby parenting our children with a greater degree of empathy, especially since we have now walked in both pairs of shoes.

Why Don't You Do It This Way?

While growing up, when our moms would offer to teach us how to cook or clean (although sometimes it was less offering and more a verbal threat that, unless we complied, no man would want us), we would turn up our noses. And while rolling our eyes, we would reply with great disdain, but under our breaths, "I don't need to know that stuff. I'll hire someone to do it."

Our mumbled protests faded into oblivion. Undeterred in their zeal to teach us the skills needed to make us good wives for their unknown sons-in-law, they commanded our attention by taking us by the hand and showing us how to scrub the toilet or how to sort the laundry by color "the right way," that is, *her* way.

We also had to listen to our mothers' mantras about picking up after ourselves, keeping our rooms cleaned, and keeping our drawers neat and tidy. In an effort to shame us into submission, they would repeatedly refer to us as "slobs." Of course, even if we found it in ourselves to cooperate (usually when we needed a ride or wanted to extend our curfew), our cleaning efforts never measured up to her way, "the right way." We pretty much tuned our mothers out when their tone of voice reached that whining, nagging pitch associated with the command to clean or pick up. It is thus usually a surprise when we discover that we have acquired her habits. Many of our respondents commented that it was through the act of housekeeping that they discovered their mother's presence.

Renee, who has a strained relationship with her mom, says, "I was in my first apartment and became somewhat obsessive-compulsive about cleaning it, having it look nice for others, just like my mom used to do." Jenny, the thirty-nine-year-old wine sales representative from Illinois, says, "I was in my thirties, being obsessive about keeping things organized and getting things done, remembering birthdays, doing things for others. Sometimes I feel negative about it since I'm so obsessively neat and clean around the house, just like my mom was."

This observation comes from a forty-two-year-old Hispanic, married human resources specialist from Illinois: "I was in my twenties—and it's actually comical and laughable now—when I first realized I did things like Mom. I'd put rubber bands on door knobs and save zillions of garbage bags, just like Mom. I don't think I was aware on the surface at first. The realization part is funny. I feel like we have this genetic bond!"

Who's That in the Mirror?

Relatives, family friends, and even strangers frequently gaze at children, as though seeking some long-lost treasure, trying to discover which parents' genes won out. "You have your mother's eyes." "You're the image of your mother." As little girls, some of us swelled with great pride when we heard these words, while others shrank in despair at the news. Jennifer "was always told my whole life that I resembled her physically, which I resented deeply as a child." As adults, the announcement can bring equally strong reactions. For Kathy, it was a sense of pride: "I was around nineteen, and I remember I was sitting on the floor leaning up against a coffee table, having a drink. My uncle said to my aunt, 'Who does Kathy remind you of right now?' My aunt glanced over and smiled, "Why she's an exact image of her mother.'"

Being told by others that we look like our moms garners a certain reaction, depending on how we feel about them. However, when the news is delivered by our own bodies, it feels like a Star Trek experience. Many of our respondents and interviewees saw. their mothers' hands and faces popping out of them. Virginia, a thirty-nine-year-old convenience store manager and a divorced mother of one from Ohio, says, "It's just the way she holds her left hand while she's eating with her right—a certain position. I was in my late teens when I happened to be dining with friends, looked down at my plate, glanced over to my left hand, and there it was: my mother's hand growing out of my arm. My heart went cold."

This comment comes from a forty-one-year-old closing officer from Illinois, who is married and the mother of two: "The one I remember most vividly is washing the car on a Saturday—no makeup, unwashed hair—and as I passed by the window of the car, I realized how much I looked like my mother! It was actually a bit frightening."

Miranda, the forty-eight-year-old divorced elementary school librarian from Ohio, says, "I hear myself using her vitriolic tongue, and much as I don't want to sound that way, it's as if the devil makes me do it! My dad used to say, 'Sometimes you sound just like your mother.' It's true. I look exactly like my father, but as soon as I open my mouth, what comes out is my mother! There are many times I regret it because I don't always like hearing my own voice saying things I've heard her say and not liking it then either."

Linda, the thirty-five-year-old magazine production manager from Vancouver, British Columbia, says, "At the oddest times I found myself sounding exactly like her. Some years ago I was at a party and people were discussing a particular social issues that I really didn't know anything about. In the middle of the conversation, I mindlessly began parroting an opinion of hers . . . It was as if someone snuck her brain into my body for a moment!"

Angela, the fifty-year-old interior decorator and widowed mother of three from Colorado whose mom was a great deal like the character Auntie Mame, says, "Some of my mother's traits and physical appearance are evident even from my teens to my fifties. I'm not as petite as she is but have a great deal of similar facial traits. I noticed one evening about ten years ago, when I was putting on my coat and realized my mother's hand came out. I smiled. No matter how you may think you're different, something always awakens the realization that you're not."

Angela has a point. We cannot escape from the similarities we have with our moms, whether they are actions, tone of voice, words, quirks, or our cheekbones. Nature and nurture cannot be escaped or controlled. Wandering Daughters are more likely to cringe at such talk, while Untraveled and Prodigal Daughters will smile and nod their head in agreement, feeling at peace with the conundrum of mother-daughter likeness and unlikeness.

Dancer Margie Gillis has her own unique perspective on this issue: "I really always thought that I was like my mother. I was just part of the tribe. It wasn't particularly me more than any of the other children. I just never thought that grunting the same tonal quality, or developing traits that are like your mother's traits, or discovering your hands look like the hand that you used to hold when you were a child, was anything negative. That, to me is like, 'Oh, my gosh!'" And as these words leap from her lips, her face lights up in wonderment.

Why Fight It?

For some Wandering Daughters, the "my mother/my self syndrome" is something they continue to react and fight against, thus becoming afflicted with the my mother/my unself syndrome. This reactionary position not only makes their mothers' influence all the stronger but also ties them together ever so tightly.

On a somewhat related note, even Nancy Friday, in her predominantly mother-bashing book My Mother/My Self, admits, "Looking at what mother may or may not have done so many years ago locks us into the past. She did it. There is nothing I can do about it. Blaming mother keeps us passive, tied to her. It helps us avoid taking responsibility for ourselves.... Blaming mother is just a negative way of clinging to her still." Whether it is blaming her for what she has or has not done, or blaming her for having negative qualities, we remain stuck at the crossroads of our journey.

Consider Joan Marie, a forty-five-year-old divorced computer programmer from Ohio: "I have always been terrified, and still am, that I may have some of the qualities I detest in my mother. I fight any tendencies that may be considered her traits. I do tend to be controlling and manipulative, despite my struggle against it."

For some of the respondents, these incidents of discovery are merely speed bumps, which they use as an opportunity either to reinforce those traits of their moms they see as valuable and worthwhile or to modify or extinguish the ones that are less desirable. For others, like Joan Marie, they are more like huge craters, which require a greater degree of work to overcome.

Mae, a forty-nine-year-old special education teacher and administrator, married mother of one from Illinois, first had to develop greater self-acceptance, which occurred at the height of a personal crisis:

> While I was very aware early on that we shared some likes, dislikes, and values, I think I purposely fought to see any similarities during my high school and college years. After a disastrous first marriage, I began to be more comfortable with myself and was able to really connect with my mom once again. At this point I was feeling very vulnerable yet found great inner strength, one of my mother's strongest traits. It was at this time also that I truly understood my mother's unconditional love for me and her complete support.

Getting Unstuck

Once we can stop fighting and let go of our fears and angers regarding our mothers' darker, more negative traits, we free ourselves to recognize their more positive qualities. By doing so, we humanize our mothers. They are neither all bad nor all good. They are just like the rest of the human race. And by humanizing our mothers, we neutralize the fears, angers, and resentments that have prevented us from recognizing ourselves as individuals in our own right, alike yet different from her. As Carrie says, "It was only when I had accepted the fact that she did have good qualities as well as bad ones that I could accept the ways I was both like and different from her."

Joan Marie is headed in the right direction if she can accept these qualities as part of her interactive style, detaching them from her mom. By acknowledging them as her own, it becomes less of a struggle to change those behaviors that she finds destructive in her life.

This process punctuates the return home not only to our mothers but to ourselves as well. We are no longer reacting against her, using her as a baseline in determining who we are or are not, but rather assessing ourselves in a more objective way so that we can begin capitalizing on the strengths we happen to share with her and then work toward changing those qualities we do not like. The energy we expend shifts away from a focus on her to a focus on ourselves. That can be a scary prospect for some since it means we begin looking inside and thus begin taking responsibility for who we are today.

Even though we may experience a strong mix of feelings about some of her qualities, we can still be at peace. That has happened to Robin, the thirty-eight-year-old psychologist from Colorado, who says:

> I often feel sad that she is such a shallow person, incapable of intimacy or dealing with real feelings of real people. Sad that she's lost my sister's goodwill, whom she felt closest to. Anger at her selfishness and tendency to withdraw and withhold when she's displeased. But the sadness outweighs the anger. Anger at the favoritism she displays toward my brother, the only male and the baby of the family. Hurt over her unequal distribution of time, energy, money, and her sentimental belongings, favoring other children over me. Glad I'm not much like her but okay with the ways that I am like her.

Looking Within

Many of our respondents found therapy to be a midwife to this process of detachment and acceptance. A forty-two-year-old single account executive from California with an M.B.A. says she was upset with her mom for not divorcing her dad, an alcoholic: "I used to really dislike being around my mom. I resented her and felt the reason I was so unhappy and dysfunctional was her fault [for not leaving my dad]. Now that I am more mature and have gone through therapy and done some reading on the subject, I realize it wasn't her fault, and I can enjoy her with or without her faults."

For other respondents whose moms suffered from more serious emotional problems, seeking therapy was particularly helpful not only in coming to terms with their moms' erratic behaviors, but also in dealing with their own personal issues. Says Martha, the forty-year-old "child-free" married journalist from Ohio whose mom suffers from mental illness and has herself been diagnosed as manic-depressive, "I spent my thirties doing my best to rid myself of any trace of her, which of course doesn't work. I was in therapy trying to find out why I was chronically depressed and suicidal." She has stopped reacting against those "traces of her mother" and sought help, which has finally led her to a stable and peaceful life. Crystal, the forty-two-year-old corporate trainer and divorced mother of one from Illinois, whose mom was agoraphobic and housebound while she was growing up, says, "I generally found I had a negative streak and was distressed. My mother sees herself as a victim. I chose not to live that unhappily and entered therapy."

Although a daughter may have characteristics similar to her mom, the path to an awareness of her own self-identity apart from her mom begins by looking within. Rather than focus on our moms' shortcomings, expending energy on what we think they could do to change and improve themselves, we need to take that same energy and channel it into positive action toward our own personal growth. Billie, the thirty-seven-year-old waitress-actress-singer from Illinois who is best friends with her mom, says, "Going through therapy helped me realize that I, like my mother, don't ask for enough. We let people walk all over us. I have been working on this part of my personality. I need to speak up for myself much more." And this observation is from Wendy, the forty-one-year-old married mother of one from Texas: "I was in my twenties when I realized I was a LOT like my mom. My memory is that of a process rather than a single event. It helped me begin to understand some of my own difficulties, and with the help of some therapy, helped me to see my ability to choose, although that is still a difficult process."

Therapy is but one way to initiate the process. Reading self-help books, participating in women's groups either formally or informally, and talking to friends all contribute to a greater degree of self-awareness. Once we are able to humanize our moms and recognize that they have some qualities we like and some that we do not like, we are in a better spot to make decisions regarding the quality of the relationship we want to have with her. For those of us whose moms have more of the qualities we value, our relationships will require lower maintenance. There will be no feelings of dread when she calls or guilt when we do not call. For those of us whose moms have more of the qualities we do not value, our relationship will require greater maintenance. These higher-maintenance mother-daughter relationships require more patience and work, depending on how much we want to put into it. It is nice to know the choice is ours.

Making the Best of It

As for those qualities in our moms that were self-defeating, negative, limiting, or interpersonally destructive, many of the respondents were able to let go of their angers and disappointments and turn these around, using them to their advantage. Jennifer, the thirty-eight-year-old retired married mother of one from Illinois who, as a Prodigal Daughter, is at peace in her relationship with her mother, says she is "an extremely happy, well-adjusted, assertive adult. I'm sure I owe a great deal of this to my mother because I saw so clearly everything she did wrong and made sure to do the opposite. I don't belittle or scream at my husband. Her hypochondria made me never even take aspirin. I've always had a career, so I don't depend on others for my own life. I've traveled extensively as opposed to her fears of leaving."

Some of our respondents learned the perniciousness of racism and bigotry through their mothers' ignorance. Shirlee, a thirty-nine-year-old homemaker and mother of three from Texas, says, "Even though I respect and appreciate my mother, she is not without her flaws. She grew up in a time when it wasn't acceptable to socialize with black people, and I still see racism in her everyday life. This has become a very sensitive area where my niece is concerned, and they've had many heated arguments on this subject. I will never have her opinions of any race of people just because of their skin."

Cassie shares an interesting perspective on how her mother has helped her: "Mother raised us to believe that family was one of the most important values, yet our family isn't at all close. I feel my own husband and children have a close and supportive family structure, so perhaps I inherited the value from mother but learned different techniques to foster it." This notion of different techniques in regard to the values our mothers taught is a crucial awareness in the journey back to her. If we can dig past those techniques, as Cassie has, down to the core values, we are in a much better spot to appreciate the heart of what our mothers offered us. Colette, a consultant, teacher, and mother of four, was able to do this with her mom: "While she always did so in a very negative way, she was clear about where she stood on things. That clarity of position and willingness to be open about my position is a value I hold and live every day. However, I have learned how to be strong without being negative or abrasive."

Some daughters, after digging past the techniques, found there was nothing to be found. That is the case with Gwen, the forty-seven-year-old married photographer from Ohio who has become her mom's primary caretaker. As she was growing up, she had to fill the voids left by her mother's extreme aloofness and distance:

> There were lots of times in my life, in my adult life mostly, that I just wish I had a whole different mother. Sometimes I met older women, and I'd say to myself, "I wish I had a mother like that": like someone who took dance classes and who took yoga—you know all the

things that I thought were interesting and people who were expressive and warm and loving, and I would say to myself, "You can get to know these people, but they are not your mother. You just know them as people, and you've got the mother you've got and you know that she's not going to change.

Gwen took her mother's weaknesses and decided she would have to teach herself those things that her mother was not able to:

She doesn't do too much spontaneously, and for me that's one of the first things I had to learn when I left her nest—to live spontaneously and not to be afraid to trust people and to feel that it was okay and to have real empathy for people and to really connect with people. I didn't really learn that from her. I really felt that having the mother I had, it was a challenge for me to find warmth in my own life and to create it. I don't blame her. Her mother was probably more aloof than she was. She was an only child and grew up in a totally different, stiff environment, and she did the best she could. I have had conversations with both of my sisters about this. And we all wish we had someone else, and we just had to go out and create it—and we did. You know my aunt says to me, "God, I don't know how you and your sisters grew up in the straightest family and yet how you all did such interesting things in your lives." It was sort of that we HAD to. It was survival for us. Where it came from, I don't know.

And so from Gwen's perspective, her relationship with her mother "has been one of the biggest challenges of my life. To transcend her fears, her unemotionality, her lack of warmth and communication skills. All this I had to reconfigure/create for myself—and not to blame her for it but accept her and try to teach her what I have learned. And be willing to have to be her mother now."

Gwen best illustrates the Prodigal Daughter's journey back home. By taking her mother's weaknesses as a challenge, she was able to carve out a life of meaning and fulfillment for herself without sacrificing her relationship with her mom. Rather than cling to angers and resentments over what her mother failed to give her, Gwen has been able to appreciate how these inadequacies have made her life experiences so much richer. Because of her ability to forgive her mom and be compassionate toward her, she is now able to reconnect with her and give her the gift of herself.

When asked if at this point in their lives they respect and value their mothers, a whopping 81 percent of our respondents answered affirmatively. When asked if they respect the differences between themselves and their moms and if they value many of her qualities, 72 percent responded affirmatively, 16 percent responded negatively stating they did not want to be anything like her, and 12 percent answered that they did not care one way or the other.

It is hard to say what comes first: accepting her, which frees us to be more self-accepting, or the other way around. Regardless of the sequence, there seems to be a greater degree of peace among Prodigal and Untraveled Daughters regarding these similarities and differences. That is not to say that they belong to the Best Friends Club or do not experience anger and frustration at what their moms might say or do—or that they necessarily spend a lot of time with their moms. Much like gold diggers, with deep faith and tremendous resolve, they just keep sifting through the dirt until they see the precious yellow metal.

My Son Is My Son 'Til He Gets Him a Wife, But My Daughter's My Daughter All Her Life

9

*I just wish my mom knew the absolute worst about
me and still loved me the way she does now. Maybe
she does know in her heart but doesn't want to
acknowledge it. Or is that kind of relationship even
possible with a mother? Is that what friends are for?*

Jeanine, forty-five-year-old waitress from California

In any of the usual gathering places frequented by women—restaurants, tennis or aerobics classes, office lunchrooms, the soccer field—when one of them announces in casual conversation that she and her mom are "best friends," immediate reactions from the other women in the group will vary. Some will lock eyes with her, firmly nod their heads, and smile a smile that can only be understood by those who are members of the "My Mom Is My Best Friend Club." Others heave a deep sigh and at the very pit of their stomach feel either a profound sadness or a burning anger. So as not to have their grief or jealousy detected, they cast a glance into a space of a memory and, with a half nod and a limp smile, appear to be interested in the conversation. And then there are others, who, while listening politely with the appropriate amount of eye contact and head nods, have a jumble of thoughts bumping around in their heads trying to sort out why anyone in the world would want to be best friends with her mother!

The Best Friends Club

Moms as best friends is a controversial topic among boomer daughters. When asked if mothers and daughters should be best friends, the conversations with our interviewees became animated, thoughtful, and emotional. Judge Susan Dlott says, "No, I don't think so. It's a different type of relationship. I would tell another woman my innermost feelings, but not my mother, because she's my mother. I still want to be the perfect child for her."

For some respondents, being best friends with one's mother crosses over the line into a space that should be filled by others. This is what one respondent, a forty-one-year-old closing officer and the married mother of two from Illinois, thinks: "It's important to be friends, but I don't know about best friends. I mean, I consider my husband to be my best friend, and I don't think I would feel comfortable having a best friend relationship with my mother. There are certain things about your life that your mother doesn't have to know. I mean you can be friends, but not best friends. That goes over the line."

Ellie, the culinary consultant from Chicago, agrees:

> I don't think mothers and daughters need to be best friends. Maybe when you're older, it's nice. But I still kind of hold my mother as my mother. I don't consider her my best friend; I consider her a woman who could help me throughout my life. I hold her in different respect than I do a friend. I would never call my mother "Mary." She's Mom, Mother, or Mommy. That's who she is. We've just never had that sort of relationship. And I don't see too many of my friends, both older and younger, having that type of relationship. I think it's very rare. For my circle of friends and business acquaintances, it's not there.

Dancer Margie Gillis agrees (her mom is the skier and golfer; she is the dancer): "I'm of the 'no best friends' thing. I need friendship from my mom, but not a buddy system. I don't want to play golf, and she doesn't want to come and do half the things in the world I live in. We're very different."

Untraveled Daughters are more likely to have had this type of connection from the very beginning, as is the case with one thirty-nine-year-old married educator from California: "We've always been best friends. I often just want to check in with her or share something trivial. I may need her advice on something major like relationships or finances or her instructions on something minor like sewing or cooking."

Hurdles to Jump to Friendship

There are so many factors, the majority of which are out of our control, that can influence whether a mother and daughter can be friends, let alone best friends—factors like birth order for the daughter and her female siblings, the quality of the relationship between mom and dad, mom's marital status (divorce, abandonment, or death of a dad), and degree of mental and physical health. Each one of these can serve to foster or discourage the growth of a friendship between mothers and daughters. In addition, friendship requires common interests and compatible personality types.

Janis, mother of five and a career counselor from Illinois, found the Meyers-Briggs personality test particularly enlightening about the great differences between hers and her mother's personalities: "That opened up a whole world for me. First of all, I discovered that I have a feeling preference in the way that I make decisions and deal with the world. My focus is on people and harmony. My mother has a strong thinking preference, which keeps her focused on the logic of a situation. I was finally able to see that we are psychologically opposite." In making this discovery, Janis was able to move toward a greater level of acceptance of her mom and herself.

Last but not least, a mutual desire and a willingness to work at the relationship complete the picture. Although we cannot control our moms' interest and commitment, we can our own. We have to decide what is realistic given who each of us is and then either work at it or let it be.

Given the complexity of human relationships and the human condition, it is easy to see why not every mother-daughter relationship can achieve this level of intimacy. Many mothers and daughters, however, think these types of relationships just happen naturally, and when they do not, they tend to feel cheated, angry, and resentful because they cannot connect at this level and frequently blame each other for what is lacking.

Friendship with our moms, like all other relationships, requires hard work. Building a less conflicted, more harmonious, intimate relationship with our moms is part of the joy in returning home to her. This is one of the greater challenges we face at midlife, if we so choose.

Ignorance Is Bliss

One of the key ingredients in being able to cultivate a friendship requires the ability to tolerate differences and resolve conflicts. Can we freely share our feelings, thoughts, and opinions good or bad, without fear of judgment or rejection from our moms? In other words, can we have differing thoughts, values, feelings, or opinions and still maintain our connection? Can we agree to disagree and still maintain equilibrium in the relationship?

The answer appears to be a resounding "No!" Our respondents and interviewees generally comment that there is a superficiality in their relationships with their moms. This seems to be true for the most part for Wandering Daughters, Untraveled Daughters, and Prodigal Daughters. Sharing deep emotions as well as those issues and topics that could lead to conflict, disapproval, or hurt feelings is often avoided, just so we can keep peace between us.

What makes this superficiality rather perplexing is that boomer women have been typically characterized as tough and rebellious, a generation that has had the chutzpah to break into male-dominated professions and jobs ranging from engineering to construction work. And yet, when it comes to our moms, we tend to keep secrets about ourselves or about our children that would provoke her disapproval (some women still do not smoke or drink in front of their moms!). A forty-one-year-old travel agent, married and the mother of two from California, says of her mom, "She frequently tells me I'm like a best friend. I don't say the same back because of the many secrets I have kept from her over the years, mostly about men, drugs, and other things that might upset or disappoint her."

In some cases, it is our mothers who would rather we keep some of our past tucked away out of sight. Margie Gillis wishes "I could be more open about things that happened to me during the horrible seventies that I could share with her now. She very seriously says, 'Do not tell me. I don't want to know. Believe me: ignorance is bliss. I don't want to hear this, I don't want to hear this!' I would like to share it, but she doesn't want it!"

As Karen Kain says, "There are things mothers and daughters don't need to know about each other." And for that matter, they may not even want to know. Given the revolutionary waves of drug use and sexual freedom that we rode in our youth, we may sometimes feel guilty about that life of long ago and feel a need to confess these incidents to our moms.

Walking on Eggshells

Putting the secrets of our past life aside and being able to communicate openly and freely is essential to a friendship and is something boomer daughters feel is missing with their moms. In responding to a question on communication, only 6 percent of our respondents said they disagree openly with their mothers, 16 percent said they still have silent wars, 39 percent say they rarely disagree and even though 45 percent said they communicate pretty openly about disagreements, their unsolicited comments along with our conversations revealed a strong contradiction in these results, which, with varying shades, echo Kathy's comment. A forty-nine-year-old computer instructor from Minnesota, married and the mother of two, she says, "I find it hard to believe that in all these many years, I can never remember having an argument with my mother. We have great discussions—solving all the world's problems during many of them—but we do not verbally disagree or argue; we've always just silently accepted our differences."

The vast majority of women shared that there was a guardedness in their communication with their moms, particularly about their ability to be, as one respondent says, "open about the really big stuff," or this from another respondent: "We chat pleasantly and rarely discuss anything that would create an argument."

This avoidance of sharing feelings does not always have to be about conflicts but can include emotions of vulnerability as well. Judge Dlott wishes for more intimacy in her relationship with her mom: "I wish that we could talk more about feelings. In my family, people didn't verbally express feelings for each other. They expressed feelings by deed but not by words. It's totally impossible to articulate completely what I feel for my mom. I wish there were a way that I could express to her how much I love her!!" In describing the overall relationship with her mom, Judge Dlott says:

> I don't remember ever not getting along with my mother. If we had a disagreement, it was minor. I don't remember in my entire life ever having a major disagreement about my mother with anything. And the method of conflict resolution in our house, or handling conflict, was that we stopped talking to each other. Everybody stopped talking; nobody ever raised their voices. So if we did disagree about something, we just stopped talking to each other for a little while—like a day or half a day. But I don't recall any period of my life where I haven't talked to her very often and where we ever haven't agreed on anything in the least bit major. It's always been an incredibly harmonious relationship.

Generally if a relationship has not been able to tolerate disagreements and conflicts openly, it will also have difficulty handling the expression of almost any emotion. This is not an unusual dynamic in the Untraveled Daughter's relationship with her mom. Not wanting to hurt or upset our moms or ourselves often results in unshared feelings, both good and not so good.

No Boat Rocking, Please

In fairness to ourselves and our moms, the deficiency in this area for both of us has to do with our psychology. In her book, *In a Different Voice*, Carol Gilligan discusses a study that set out to discover whether there are sex differences in the games children play. She found that boys work to resolve a dispute when a conflict arises, whereas girls who are facing a conflict will terminate the game. The relationship takes precedence over the activity. Thus, women typically sacrifice winning the argument or even initiating a conflict in order to preserve the connection. Further, women avoid making clear and direct statements about their opinions or thoughts when they believe that such clarity could not only possibly make the other person in the relationship uncomfortable but also expose the differences between them. This exposure could fracture the connection, thus signaling a possible failed relationship—something women will avoid at all costs. The stakes are much higher when conflicts surface with our moms than with other relationships.

We have very different and much higher expectations of our moms than we do of our friends when it comes to accepting, tolerating, and handling the differences between us. As Janis says, "It goes into this whole big pot of idealizing mothers and wanting them to be everything to everyone. It irritates me in a way, because now that I'm a mother, it's just one more thing to be blamed for. Mothers are expected to be so much more than the humans we are." Perhaps if we could lower these expectations and see each other as just two women from different generations, we might be able to begin the work of being friends.

Many of our relationships with our moms are functioning at a fairly superficial level, untested by any open conflicts, differences, or genuine sharing of deeper feelings—that is, unless we push them or they push us. This is not just a shortcoming on our mom's part, but one on ours as well, since we too have difficulty facing conflict in our relationship with her.

In wanting to please her and avoid hurting her, we do not wish to risk disapproval because when we get it, we tend to doubt ourselves, as in the case of Mary Margaret, a forty-three-year-old sales representative and mother of two, who says, "I often find myself wondering how my mother would react in a particular situation and if I'm behaving in the way that she would. I really crave, even at my age, her approval! She's asked me many times why I need to be validated by her. I don't know; I respect her I guess. It's my way of knowing I'm doing the right thing, if she approves. Ridiculous!"

Equalizing the Relationship

Another key ingredient in establishing a friendship with our moms has to do with equality and acceptance. Relationships between parents and children are characterized by what Jean Baker Miller calls "temporary inequality." That is, parents have more to give and consequently are "superior" in that they have characteristics, experience, and abilities that are to be imparted to the "lesser" person, the child, in the relationship. The ultimate task and goal of the relationship is for the parents to engage the child in such a way as to bring the "lesser" party up to full parity or equal status with the "superior" party. The disparity in the relationship is strictly temporary. Once the child reaches adulthood, both parties have to let go—the parent of some of the power and the child of dependency—thus equalizing the relationship.

Ingrid, a human resources manager, exemplifies this shift: "I can see her now as a separate individual rather than as the person who could control my life." Another of our respondents says, "Everything she says is no longer gospel. She does have her flaws." And this observation comes from Leah, a thirty-eight-year-old married free-lance writer from New York: "My mother has recently had a close brush with death. Now I sort of have to take care of her. Before last year, though, she was just mom in the same way she'd always been mom. And I called her for advice about everything. She seemed to know everything! Every once in a while, I'd say to myself, 'Wait, you're a grown-up too!'"

This issue of equality is one that boomer daughters and their mothers grapple with the most. Wandering Daughters and some Untraveled Daughters tend to maintain a relationship of unequal sta-tus with their moms but for different reasons. Wanderers, by contin-uing to focus on her failures and inadequacies, keep themselves stuck in the roles of children and still trying to "fix" mommy so they can be happy. Thus, they unwittingly empower their mothers to rule their lives, even if only indirectly. The same is true for some Untraveled Daughters, the only difference being that they focus on their moms' perfection, idealizing her and keeping her high up on a pedestal, blind to any of her flaws. This too keeps them stuck as children forever at her feet. Unequal mother-daughter relationships can be filled with a potpourri of emotions, including anger, resentment, and guilt, and are frequently driven by a pervasive sense of obligation and duty. One forty-five-year-old mother of two puts it this way: "I get crazy with myself when she seems to have the ability to get me to do something I really don't want to do, so she doesn't get mad." A thirty-six-year-old social worker and mother of one says, "I feel as if I must talk to her daily and fill her in on the minutiae of my life and have her share hers with me. When I don't talk to her. I feel guilty."

Consider Carol Ann, a Wandering Daughter, whose relation-ship with her daughter is totally different when it comes to sharing feelings (something she inversely learned from her relationship with her mother). Carol Ann, like many other Wandering Daughters, continues functioning in her relationship with her mom out of a sense of duty or obligation:

I see her as a very self-centered person who won't change her life but wants a say in everyone else's. She still tries to tell me how to run my life and raise my children. I talk to her every day but am relieved when the call is over, like it's just another chore I had to do that day. I dislike having to go see her because all I hear are complaints and gripes. I'm always happy when I'm driving away. I'm really a hypocrite because I'm sure she doesn't really know how I truly feel. We argue, but to keep the peace, I keep calling her.

This type of relationship, where she and her mom continue to maintain a parent-child tie, can only continue to fuel guilt, anger, and resentments, thereby promoting depression for Carol Ann.

Risky Business

If we are able to rearrange our relationship with our moms from an unequal one, where she is still functioning as the superior member and we as the lesser, to a relationship of equality, we are in a much better position to increase the level of intimacy between us and also feel a greater connection to our own self. Seeking her approval or avoiding her disapproval no longer drives the relationship, since, as an equal, she has no more power than we do. This process requires a reciprocal action on her part, which involves cooperating with the shift and accepting her daughter as an equal partner in the relationship. Some moms have difficulty relinquishing the mother-as-parent role and need some help, as Janis's mom does. Janis says:

Well, I really just wish we could talk more about feelings. I'd like to tell her just how bad I feel right now, during this long period of grieving that I'm going through, and would hope that she would empathize instead of correct me and say, "Why would you feel that way? You should've known that it was going to be this way. Don't let those people bother you." And I will stop her and say, "Mom, I don't want you to give me a lecture; I would like you to just try to understand, and if you can't, then just let me vent." And so she'll do that, but I have to give her some coaching. And I wish that I could let my hair down with her like I could a good friend—a good friend who is empathic, not someone who wants to fix or correct me.

Of course, in fairness to our moms, we often have just as much of a problem in relinquishing the daughter-as-child role by wanting to "fix or correct" her so she can measure up to our standards. Or as Virginia, retail manager and mother of one, says, "I accept her better now, not expecting her to somehow 'shape up.'"

She Is Who She Is

Poet Pat Mora, in talking about how she had to adjust to her mom's changing lifestyle, remembers that when her mother "slowed down almost to a halt, it was hard on me since that has to do more with my values. I really value activity and doing things, and it's just not her value." When Pat's mother, a very active woman who was quite involved with her kids when they were growing up, faced an empty nest, she decided to live her life on her terms. "My mom doesn't get out of bed until 3:00 in the afternoon. When my daughter got married, my mom didn't go. She said, 'Well, honey, you know I can't be up.' Now that's amazing for someone who was a devoted mother and grandmother. So I said to my sister, 'Well, you know if she doesn't want to go, why make big deal of it?' It was fine with me. I said to my mom, 'Well, you know someone's taking a video and you're going to love it,' and she will, and that's okay."

Pat is able to let her mother make her own decisions, even those she might not agree with. This was a process and took some work on Pat's part, including taking a step back in the relationship:

She sleeps until three. It drives me crazy. After my dad died, I began to nag her. I thought, "This is just no way to end your life, Mom." I felt that I was nagging for all the right reasons: that she was shortening her life span, she was not getting exercise, she's not getting daytime stimulation. I thought, "Mom, this isn't good for you." And so I was just on her. And I knew it was a detriment to our relationship. Then I realized something: one of the things that I am so grateful for in my parents is that they really gave me my life. If I had wanted to have been a nun, I would've been a nun. When I decided to get a divorce out of the church, that was fine, and when I decided to leave the university administration, that was fine. So I thought, "Okay, she did it for you. This is her life. If this is how she wants to spend it, then you have to let her and not talk about it anymore."

Pat has been able to let go and recognize that her mother can freely choose to live her life any way that she wants.

Acceptance is a key ingredient in a friendship and one that boomer daughters struggle with, just as Pat Mora has. Ellie, although not wanting to be best friends with her mom, talks about acceptance as the turning point in their relationship: "My mother and I have accepted each other for who we are. Throughout the years, we were very critical of each other in every way. Today we realize we're both two very different individuals and don't need to express our differences to each other. I never thought we would come to the acceptance of each other that has occurred. I realize today how much of the negative energy we both emitted toward each other was a waste of our precious time together. She told me one day we would be friends, and we finally are."

Some of our respondents' mothers taught them about acceptance and tolerance. Alice, a mother of three from California, thanks her mother for this: "My mother has shown me tolerance, particularly for family members who have different ideas and values. She has told me that if you don't accept people for who they are, you usually end up losing them. I will never be as nonjudgmental as my mother, but I am learning to be more accepting."

Birds of a Feather

Another ingredient needed in maintaining a friendship has to do with shared values, common interests, and similar lifestyles, all of which pose a special challenge to boomer daughters and their moms, given the discrepancy in opportunities available to both generations.

Carrie, the forty-six-year-old business owner from Ohio, posed an interesting question: "I love that I am less critical and more accepting of my mother at this stage in my life and she of me. I sense, however, that my mother wishes her life had been different and is not always willing to accept the choices she has made. I know she is envious of what she thinks my life is, and I wonder if many mothers of her generation who had fewer opportunities, support systems, and choices are both happy for and envious of their daughters."

Given that mothers are prone to human emotions like jealousy or envy, it would certainly seem normal for them to feel a twinge of rivalry with their daughters who have surpassed them. Mothers would have a hard time admitting this precisely because of the cultural expectations of the "good-enough" mother. Daughters can sometimes experience guilt feelings in having achieved more, professionally and economically, than their moms, a situation that can leave them both with uncomfortable feelings that are too difficult to share.

Furthermore, it is difficult for mothers to understand and relate to the lifestyle their daughters lead. This can be a particular challenge when it comes to "bringing home the bacon," since they have little or no experience in being able to survive in the work world of the nineties. Daughters frequently have to seek out other support systems and mentors when problems at work arise. Thus, there are some parts of their daughters' lives that our moms cannot fully share. This can adversely affect whether a friendship could blossom.

This is the case for Jane, a forty-three-year-old Hispanic attorney and a married mother of three from Kentucky: "I always knew my mother and I were different. I always worked, had a job. I always wanted a degree, to be dependent on myself. My mother was a homemaker, where I was career oriented. We share family focus and orientation, but not much else."

Some of our respondents talked about how their moms wanted to be friends with them, but it was too late in the asking. Marie, a forty-five-year-old widowed registered nurse and the mother of three from Illinois, says of her mom, "She is elderly and has medical problems. I think about her possibly dying. I feel cheated at times with our relationship not being good. My mother didn't really socialize much with me. Now that she's elderly and alone, she wants to be my buddy, and I can't. I don't have that type of feeling toward her. I respect her because she's my mother. I'm no longer angry at her. This is resolved. She probably did the best she could raising me and my sister and brother."

Friendships take time, energy, and lots of work. It is more difficult to form such a connection later in the mother-daughter relationship, but not impossible. Equalizing our relationships with our moms in some ways can serve to promote a type of friendship between us, if that is what we both want. But like all other friendships, both parties have to be willing to work at it in order for the connection to be a viable relationship.

Becoming the Equalizer

Many of our survey respondents have discovered the tools of assertiveness, setting limits, and establishing boundaries as essential ingredients in developing and maintaining an equal relationship with our moms. Lila, a forty-five-year-old singer-songwriter and a divorced mother of three from Illinois, says, "I as a woman see her as a woman now, and not just my mother. I understand her views on things more, although I don't necessarily agree with them. When her views affect me, I can now speak up for myself. Therefore, I'm not harboring things like I used to have to do. I don't let her negativism affect me like it used to."

Ballerina Karen Kain says of her mom, "There were times when I'd have to take a deep breath and avoid arguing about some things because she just wouldn't understand." When asked how she learned to let go with her mom, Karen replies:

> That took time. It took time to create the boundaries that made it clear that I was an adult and that now I had to run my own life. Some part of her and some part of me wanted me to remain a child. But that transition where she had to let me go and I had to want to be let go took a long time to happen. It took time for me to learn that I could actually set some boundaries and that she would instinctively understand. That was a really valuable thing. If your mother really loves you and she really wants to be in your life and feels that what she's doing is threatening you, you just have to let her know how far she can go. I found that that works on any number of relationships. I find places where it's not important to stand my ground and other places where it is.

Janis also speaks up to her mom:

> I talked to her over the weekend, and she said, "Jan, they're just so *Italian*." And I said to her, "Mom, what does *that* mean? Would you tell me please?" And I could tell she was embarrassed because I put her on the spot,

and she paused and said something very tactful: "Well, it means they are hard workers, and they are kind of noisy, and they aren't really into culture." And you know she was picking her words after that. About five or six years ago, I decided that I am not going to bite my tongue when I hear this kind of crap. And so I take kind of a teasing tone to her, but I decided not to let it go by because I don't let anybody else get by with it.

Equalizing the relationship with our moms can be fully successful only if our mothers are able to adapt to the changing balance of power, as Aileen's mom has been able to do. Aileen was the respondent who was very disturbed when she found out that she was pregnant with a girl. She called her mom with the news, telling her that she did not want to "perpetuate another agonizing mother-daughter relationship for a third generation." Aileen talks of her mother's reaction: "My mother was quiet. Then she calmly said, 'If you feel so strongly, why don't you just have an abortion?' I shut up instantly, taken aback. Then I said, 'Uh, I'll call you back later.' And in an instant, she had managed to put things in perspective. I didn't have to perpetuate a relationship like we had, or like my mom had with her mother. I could do it differently." Rather than take Aileen's feelings to heart and become defensive or revert to a "parent" role and admonish her for these feelings, Aileen's mom remained detached, which then allowed Aileen to evaluate the situation objectively.

A few other respondents commented on their moms' ability to refrain from interfering. Marianne, a forty-two-year-old human resources specialist, appreciates her mother's ability "to advise but not interfere. I still don't know how she does it, but she makes me feel that she cares, gives her input, and then just butts out."

Equalizing the Terminator

Some moms, because of complex reasons, the most pervasive of which is extremely low self-esteem, are simply unable to give unsolicited advice. Cassie, a teacher from Alberta, recalls that her mother "bullied me into compliance, and I let her. It was so much easier than to stand up to her and deal later on with the tight-lipped silences and the guilt." Cassie goes on to talk about how differently she and her mom view the "closeness" in their relationship, a phenomenon not uncommon among boomer daughters:

> I believe there's a difference between my relationship with my mother and hers with me. I think she would say that the relationship is closer than I would. My mother is very controlling and passive-aggressive, to use a bit of the jargon. My philosophy is to go along to get along, so I acquiesce most of the time. Mother is dogged, and I found the path of least resistance to be what worked with her. Because the relationship went smoothly, she would say it was close, but I felt she wanted too much ownership of me. She could have the surface, the external responses she wanted, but my differences I kept to myself.

Trying to equalize this relationship had its frustrations for Cassie:

> Any attempts over the years, when I wanted to establish a more equal relationship, mother would feel threatened and end up sulking and saying, "You're picking on me." What I did instead of persisting was to continue to avoid issues. I became a little better and am still learning to be detached. Unfortunately, this also means being detached from a supportive relationship. Now, she is eighty-two and is less and less connected to me, and I don't know how to reconnect unless it's again a parent-child relationship. I think it would be cruel to try to reinvent our relationship at this stage when it would only be confusing for her and not productive. It's always been difficult for her to see a need for change as anything but criticism.

Many of our other respondents had the same frustrations as Cassie in trying to equalize the relationship with their moms. Sophie, a thirty-seven-year-old fundraiser and mother of two stepchildren, says, "I respect and love my mother as a daughter. I wish we could be more like friends, but I don't think it'll ever happen. Because she doesn't respect the lines I've drawn, I feel more comfortable in a long-distance relationship with her. I keep wondering when I'll be able to reach beyond myself and let her be my friend. And then I wish she would respect the limits I set. I wish I could allow her to be my friend, yet I'm not able to do so."

For Leah the equalizer problem looks like this:

> Recently my little sister remarked that our mother is her best friend (they live in the same city). I feel, too, that my mother has the possibility of being my best friend, if only she would stop being so judgmental of me and accept the fact that I'm an adult who has made different decisions. At the same time, I realize I am overly judgmental of the decisions she has made! My task is to make peace with this, and to recognize and accept that she may or may not make peace on her own part.

Leah's new insight may begin the process of equalizing her relationship with her mom. Many daughters want their moms simply to accept and approve everything they do, and when their moms express their own differing viewpoints, the daughter is the one who keeps her in the parent role by demanding that she agree with her! These women are all in a difficult spot. They have to accept that their relationship with their mom, at least at this time, cannot grow beyond its parent-child tie. This is a loss in both the mothers' and daughters' lives, one that is frequently lamented by daughters. Says Martha, a journalist: "I see other mother-daughter relationships that are full of joy and friendship. I'm sad for what I will never have."

Esther, a nurse and mother of four from Kentucky, is grateful she had a close relationship with her mom, "especially when I see so many women who don't. It appears to be such a loss, an emptiness."

In most cases, equalizing the relationship takes an act of courage, a willingness to risk breaking the old parent-child tie and refashioning it into a mutual, reciprocal woman-woman tie. This part of the journey is marked with intensified conflicts and disagreements as the new boundaries are established. And as with anything that is new, the refashioned connection is fragile and for a time requires a vigilance to be strengthened and maintained. This process takes even more vigilance when the mother is unable to reciprocate and continues to hold on to her power base.

Equalizing Tools and Strategies

Prodigal Daughters and some Untraveled Daughters tend to see their moms more realistically, warts and all. They have been able to view their mothers contextually, through the lens of compassion. They can still experience feelings of guilt or anger within the relationship, but with much less intensity. This does not mean that these daughters necessarily have closer relationships with their moms, although it might. Generally it does mean that they are able to choose their battles wisely, as in Karen Kain's case, or decide if they choose to battle at all, as in Cassie's situation. They tend to see their moms as women with no greater or lesser power than their own within the relationship. And even if their moms are not able to cooperate with the shift, they continue to maintain their sense of adulthood by utilizing various strategies to communicate and to detach when necessary, and by doing so, they are much less likely to feel resentment. Although these strategies may not necessarily be considered effective communication skills from an assertiveness perspective, they work with moms who have difficulty participating in the change of status.

Some daughters make the conscious decision to refrain from arguing and to focus on the positive aspects of the relationship, like

Renee, the Wandering Daughter who transformed into a Prodigal Daughter in our group discussion: "It remains strained at times. I keep my mouth shut more, but I tend to see my mother as an unhappy person with few friends, who lacks an adventurous spirit. She remains quite critical of my taste in clothes, furnishings, and other areas. However, she loves her grandchildren and me, and I realize she shows it primarily by cooking for us, cleaning, and yes, even rearranging my belongings!"

Jennifer, a thirty-eight-year-old mother of two, keeps the time spent with her mom short and sweet: "I'm at peace in my relationship with her now since we only see each other one to two times a year. If the visits get too long, she starts in again, and all that old anger comes up, though we never fight. I let her keep the controls. I think she wishes things were better and sometimes pretends they are."

Other daughters have found creative solutions to the task of simply enjoying their moms. Animal rights activist Terri Crisp takes the best of her mom by telephone: "My mom and I do so much better on the phone than we do face to face talking to one another. I mean, we can get on the phone and can talk for hours. Put us in the car for two hours, and we don't even come close to saying nearly as much, and certainly it's not as much an open conversation. If we have something really important to talk about, we don't do it in person; we do it by phone."

This comment is from a librarian: "Mostly I either do what she wants, distract her with humor, or get quietly stubborn."

Some daughters discovered that a change in their approach resulted in a reciprocal change on the part of their moms, as with this housewife: "Over the years, I've learned to change my approach rather than be frustrated by what I perceived to be stubbornness. My growing gentleness of approach made me more aware of her patience and consistency."

Colette, a forty-nine-year-old married mother and consultant and teacher from Illinois, handles her mom this way: "She focuses only on what's wrong in her life, not what's right, and she'll do the same with my life if I give her the information to do so. I'm careful to share only the positives, never the difficult times. I would never ask for advice."

These women have discovered that by limiting contact, surrendering certain battlegrounds, and selectively sharing, they can maintain some level of connection with their moms. They are fully accepting of what the relationship is, given who their mothers are and what they are capable of, and they have stopped trying to make the relationship be something it cannot be. In other words, they have accepted that they cannot put a square peg in a round hole.

Much like alcoholics who finally surrender and admit powerlessness, then are able to forgive themselves and move on with their lives, daughters must also surrender; by their letting go and forgiving, the seeds of a more connected relationship will be planted. For some, this may result in a depth once thought impossible; for others, it may result in being able to connect at new level, even if only sporadically. The relationship can be enjoyed for what it can give.

Janis says it best: "Since I can't change her, I should find ways to delight in her."

10

You'll Never Miss the Water 'Til the Well Runs Dry, and You'll Never Miss Your Mother 'Til She's Gone

Maybe that's what life expects us to do: be responsible for each other regardless of the labels. Who is the mother? The one who can be, I guess.
Cassie, forty-nine-year-old artist and teacher from Alberta

Y ou're not leaving this house without a jacket!" "It's going to snow today; take your boots." Great wars were fought when these commands were issued from the lips of our mothers. And after we groaned and argued, begged and pleaded, we always capitulated but usually only after she issued what dancer Margie Gillis calls the "Mother's Curse." If Margie did not wear her boots in the cold Montreal winter, she usually paid for it, and her mother predicted the results: "If you don't, you'll catch pneumonia!"

This was the final blow and temporarily quelled our protestations. As Margie says, "If she caught me going out the door not wearing enough clothes, she'd say, 'You'll catch pneumonia!' It would never fail: I would catch a cold! But if I got out the door without her seeing me, I'd be fine."

And so, given the power of the Mother's Curse, we capitulated (but never totally), and as we begrudgingly whipped our jacket from its hanger or yanked our ugly, dirty boots from the corner of the closet, we mumbled our disdain for her as we walked out the door.

The Magic of Jell-O and Soft-Boiled Eggs

We did not protest all of her attempts to nurture and protect us, just when it interfered with what we wanted to do. When we were sick and in pain, however, we were much more cooperative with her demands. (Of course, she was much more sympathetic in issuing them. Mother's Curse transformed itself into Mother's Blessing.) We learned that through each and every episode of illness that befell us, she could almost always make us feel better. One of our respondents recalls:

> You know, she was always there when I was sick. I told her the other day I had such an excruciating migraine headache last week that I had to go to the hospital and get a shot. And she was upset. "Why didn't you call us? Daddy and I would have driven right to Columbus" [from Dayton, about seventy-five miles away]. And she means it! She was really hurt that I didn't call her instead of having my law clerk take me. But that's the way she was when we were sick. When we were little, she would sit by our bed the whole time. You know, just to hold our little hands or to put a cold cloth on our hot little foreheads, and my mother would make Jell-O. That would be the first thing she'd do is start making Jell-O and soft-boiled eggs! I don't know what multipurpose healing qualities Jell-O had, but no matter what illness we were stricken with, my mom made Jell-O, and it always seemed to make us feel better.

In talking to this respondent, we were both flooded with our own memories. I (BMc) vividly recall that when I was in elementary school, I frequently would feign illness just so I could have my mom's undivided attention, which was at its best when we were ill. There was something about being sick that felt really wonderful!

Whenever my stomachaches or headaches (real or imagined, but mostly imagined) kept me from school, my mom always made absolutely perfect soft-boiled eggs, which she would miraculously slice while in the shell (something my father taught her to do) and serve them to me on a special tray amid hugs and kisses while I lay on our living room couch mesmerized by Captain Kangaroo or Howdy Doody. All of this was definitely worthwhile, in spite of having to confess it as a lie during First Friday confessionals. I am sure Father Ted, whose queue of sinners was the longest and most often fought over among my peers (he predictably and perfunctorily gave the easiest of penances: three Our Fathers and Three Hail Marys), diagnosed the face behind the voice as a hypochondriac.

I (VWR) remember being ill more often than feigning the symptoms and how well my mother seemed to carry the role of nurse, even though she was trained as a teacher. Often I would be ill in the winter (or so I remember). Sometimes simple colds became something worse, like bronchitis or pneumonia. But even if the illnesses were simple ones that did not require hospitalization, Mum's trays of soup, toast, maybe a soft-boiled egg, and sometimes red Jell-O helped calm me and, I am quite sure, got me better sooner than I might have done otherwise. Even when I am ill now, there is no substitute for my mum and her wise nursing. When she visited me recently, I had to massage her back each night with ointment to deal with a rash she had acquired. As I stroked her back, I felt oddly as if I had become her as nurse—and that I was up to it.

This need for our mother's nurturing does not end with childhood. Judge Susan Dlott says:

> If I could have only one person with me if something serious were to happen, that person would be my mother, not my husband. Just last week, I had the day from hell. You name it, I had it on the docket. I had marijuana growers from the Wayne National Forest who both had been married to the same wife from Ashland County,

and I had an Ohio State University professor who pleaded guilty to stealing documents from the Vatican. And then there was some poor Mexican immigrant whom I had to deport for phony INS documents who sang in the church choir in Columbus twice a week. The last thing I wanted to do was to have to deport this poor kid, and you know I came back in the chambers and I thought to myself, "I want my mommy!!! I want my mommy. She can fix anything. She can make Jell-O and chicken soup and make me feel better, make everything better!!!"

For most of us, our moms have always been there for us, for as far back as our memory will take us, nurturing, caretaking, fixing, correcting, criticizing, and loving us. And then somewhere along the way, just around our midlife, we discover that we are wearing her shoes while she has mysteriously slipped into ours. For some, it is a sudden change, for others a much more gradual one. A forty-two-year-old business owner and mother of three from Nebraska notes, "As she has gotten older our relationship has changed. Sometimes I feel I'm like she once was for me—the wise one, the encourager, the listener—and that's okay."

We now worry about her health. Over 75 percent of our respondents think about their moms daily, and when they do, their thoughts are filled with concern regarding her well-being. So at midlife we are faced with another twist in the road. This alteration often magnifies and intensifies the feelings that dominated the relationship throughout its history. For Wandering Daughters, angers and resentments swell. Untraveled and Prodigal Daughters frequently assume the role with greater ease, although not without frustration.

Premature Motherhood

For a few of our respondents, being their mother's mother began long before they were ready for the responsibility. When a mother's premature death or physical or mental illness strikes a family, usually one of the daughters takes on her mother's role. Some daughters step in without missing a beat and meet the challenge head on. My (BMc) mother was thirteen years old when her mother suddenly died, leaving my grandfather with three dependent children ranging in age from nine to thirteen. Mom, the oldest daughter, stepped up to the plate and took care of her dad and younger brother and sister. She quit school in the ninth grade to cook, clean, and tend to the family. When asked how she felt about the sacrifices she made at such an early age, she responds with puzzlement: "Sacrifice? I don't think about it that way at all. It just had to be done."

For some daughters, like Crystal, the forty-two-year-old corporate trainer from Illinois whose mom was an agoraphobic, mothering her mother cultivated feelings of anger and resentment: "My mother was agoraphobic when I was growing up. She didn't leave our house for almost eleven years. I took over her responsibilities in our household. She seemed to resent me for being capable of doing this. I'm often angry with her for being weak. She's a mean woman and very self-centered. I vow daily never to give up the control and responsibility of my life. I vowed never to make my son function as an adult [in an adult role] but to allow him to experience his childhood." Crystal, however, has not let this premature burden keep her a Wandering Daughter: "I almost completely discounted her as I was growing up. I hated hearing that she couldn't help what was happening to her. I realize now that she was what she was as a result of her own life experiences. The whole thing is sort of bittersweet. Although I have compassion and understanding, parts of me resent her. I also believe it must have been very limiting to be an adult woman in the fifties and sixties."

Carrie, the forty-six-year-old business owner from Ohio who was able to accept that her mom had both good and bad qualities, says, "I have always been both parent and child with my mother, but more parent than child. Now she is seventy-one, widowed three years ago, and needs financial and emotional attention, which my brothers for the most part do not contribute. I provide support for her in numerous ways: in her work, in her dating activities. I try to be a good listener and a positive motivator for her, especially in regard to health issues."

Angela, the Untraveled Daughter from Colorado, was also a "child" mother: "My mom was gone a great deal. I was the sensible child and stayed behind to make sure bills were paid, household chores done, younger sister taken care of, school work done, and all the other things that make up responsible duties. What a martyr!" Her mom, married and divorced three times, "strove to find true love, and this need encompassed her. I just tried to be there for her. I was my mother's mother. Despite her absences, I always knew she loved me tremendously."

Sometimes mothers' busy lives or illnesses forced their daughters to take on housekeeping duties earlier than most other people. For Cleveland politician Jane Campbell, her mother's social activism meant that she had to start meal planning and grocery shopping for the family. As Jane recalls, when she turned sixteen, her mother cut a deal with her: "She said, 'Look, here's the deal. I'll let you have the car if you take your brothers wherever they want to go. Go to the grocery store, buy the food, write a menu of what we're going to eat, put it in the refrigerator. Here's the budget we have for food. You can pick the menu, buy the food, and come home and get the dinner started.' I thought that was so cool when I was sixteen! So that's how I learned menu planning and grocery shopping."

Although other daughters might have resented this responsibility, Jane had another perspective: "It was great. I thought it was fun, and it was actually fairly risk free. If I blew it, what was she going to do? Go to the grocery store and pick something up? I'm sure I didn't do it perfectly at the start. I don't remember any major screw-ups. I do remember her making me think I could do this. We had fun with the responsibility. My brothers and I would say, 'Okay, now let's have chicken this night, pasta this night, hamburger, spaghetti,' and we thought we were so cool because we could figure what we were going to eat."

The vast majority of our survey respondents were not faced with the challenges of premature motherhood like Jane or others were. But they began mothering their moms in the later years of their lives.

Mothering Our Mothers

Stepping into our mothers' shoes presents many challenges and frustrations for boomer daughters, particularly when our mothers have not completely stepped out of them (as if she or we could ever let that completely happen!). Being the parent to her does not mean that a certain glance or a particular tone of voice would not thrust us back into time, shrinking us into that little girl of long ago. Celeste, the forty-nine-year-old therapist and a divorced mother of three from Colorado, says of her mom, "I see her more as a person and less as a role in my life. I do more parenting of her now and wish the opposite was true, but I still resent it when she tells me what to do."

For some of us, our baptism into this new role initially created feelings of confusion, as it did with Cassie and Mindy. Cassie says, "I think in many ways my mother has expected me to be her strength and consolation, to lean on me, and in fact make me the parent. Complicated. Confusing. Well, I'm a responsible person. I'm strong. Maybe that's what life expects us to do: be responsible for each other regardless of the labels. Who is the mother? The one who can be, I guess."

Cassie's answer to her own question—Who is the mother?— is a poignant one. Now we are in the position of offering the physical strength, experience, knowledge, and nurturance that once came from the other side. Equalizing the relationship takes on a different face. Where once we tried to set limits regarding our independence from her, now we are teaching her how to maintain her own independence. Other lessons include helping our moms begin the process of self-discovery. Alice, a self-employed married mother of three from California, says of her mom, "My mother moved in with me at my suggestion after she started suffering panic attacks. We have worked together with a psychiatrist and a local hospital program, and I believe she is comfortable with her new life. I find myself trying to encourage her to find out who she really is and what she really likes and wants to do and to learn to put herself first instead of automatically thinking of everyone else and what their needs might be."

For Mindy, the confusion rests in the mix of emotions she experiences: "At this time in my mother's life, I am her only friend. At times this is okay, but at times I feel guilty and depressed. At times we are the best two friends and talk openly about all subjects and problems. When I free myself and see my mother as another human being to be loved and cherished, our relationship becomes a friendship, and all guilt and depression are removed. The joy of still having her in my life is fulfilling."

Do As I Say . . .

In trying to help our moms reach some level of fulfillment or satisfaction in their lives, we can sometimes drive ourselves into a state of anxiety that only Valium could temper. Leah, who earlier spoke of her desire to be best friends with her mom, says, "I often feel a deep anxiety and impatience in regard to her, a driving impulse that goes: 'If only I could get her into therapy . . . if only I could get her to start writing again . . . if only I could get her to eat better and exercise.' And then I have to stop myself and say, 'Stop! You can't affect her life. Work on your life. Let her go.' Then I say, 'Yeah, that's fine if she were someone else, but she's your mother and etc., etc., etc."

Beyond trying to "get" her mother to do things that would make her life better, Leah also wants to teach her how to live and at the same time is struggling with how much responsibility she should take for her mom's life and well-being:

I really feel I have had to teach myself how to live. If I
followed her implicit advice, I would be bound into a very
circumscribed world by fears of various sorts. Now, in retrospect, I want to teach her how to live, too—an indica-
tion, I suppose, that my congratulations to myself are
rather premature! Unfortunately, as time goes on, I learn
more and more that the rules she lived by—"one doesn't
do that sort of thing"—should have been discounted long
ago. I am attempting now to see that we have separate
lives and that her choices needn't affect mine and, more-
over, that it is not my responsibility to salvage her life. I
feel very sad that she is old and unwell now and never did
any of the many things she was capable of.

This sadness for those experiences our mothers missed or for the
sorrows they had to face in their lifetimes haunts most boomer
daughters, as with Carrie who says, "I worry whether she has
resolved some of the issues of her terrible childhood, whether she
can see herself peacefully and clearly, whether she can sustain an
independent life, whether when she dies she will feel as if her life
has been okay."

Others worry about the strained relationships between their siblings and their moms. Regina, a thirty-seven-year-old homemaker
and married mother of two from Illinois, says, "I worry about how
my older sister doesn't have much contact with her. It makes her
very sad and upset, and I feel that." Regina's mom, age sixty-six and
a divorced mother of four, worked to support her family as a legal
secretary and after forty years is still employed as such.

Others, like Jackie, feel less sympathy for their moms but still
wish to help them blossom:

I often think about why we are so different. I work part-
time and have one child, but she still gets her barks in
about the "modern lifestyle" we live today and some of

my parenting techniques. It doesn't bother me because I think she is actually jealous of the freedom I have today. I don't really feel sorry for her, but I wish the fifties and sixties had been different for her so she could have realized her full potential. I try to build up her self-esteem and let her blossom, but she is a product of her times—too scared to make changes, to find out who she really is.

When She's Alone

We are stricken with a mix of painful feelings when it comes to seeing our moms left alone. We are torn not only by the cruelty of nature when it comes to our moms' mental and physical decay, but also when the circle of people who filled their lives constricts and more of them die or move away.

For boomer daughters who are lucky enough to have their dads still in the picture, their stress is somewhat reduced, assuming, of course, that the marriage has mellowed into some level of companionship. For Diana, there is a constant worry about her mom "because she seems so small and frail now, almost childlike. Her memory is fading a little, but Dad adores her and takes loving care of her and she of him." Others worry how their moms will cope when left widows. Says Rachelle, mother of two from Illinois: "I'm thankful my mother is still with me. I fear for her, because I don't know how she will handle things after my father is gone. They depend on each other so much I don't know how she will cope." A thirty-six-year-old social worker from Illinois has similar worries: "Now that she is beginning to show her age and cannot do what she is accustomed to, I think about her failing health and mortality. I worry about if she was to survive my father and vice versa, what their lives would be like, and how it would affect my sister's and my own."

Boomer daughters whose moms are single or widowed feel particularly burdened with worry, as does Regina who says, "Right now she's getting ready to retire. She lives by herself, and I worry about her a lot—about her being lonely, sick, or financially weak. My husband and I have invited her to live with us, but she hasn't decided yet." A homemaker and mother of four from Illinois wishes her mother would move in with her: "She gets lonely, and I wish she would find a decent male partner to care for and nurture her."

We are often drawn to fill the hole of her loneliness. A forty-four-year-old teacher from Illinois says, "I worry about her since my father died three years ago. I call to see how she is feeling and chat about what she did during the day. I tell her about work, my husband, friends, and other things."

The Circle of Sacrifice

As many of the respondents talked about the role reversal in their relationship with their moms, we were especially struck by what boomer daughters are willing to sacrifice for their mothers emotionally and economically. Lily, mother of three and a singer-songwriter, says, "I just know at some point her future will rest in my hands. I'm the only child who sees her. I've always been the one to take care of her needs: trips to doctors, shopping for clothes and shoes. She spends every holiday at my home. I've been told since I was a kid, 'When something happens to Mom, she'll have to live with you.' So unless I have a secure future, I know she won't have one either." Lily has three other siblings, two of them sisters.

Gwen, the forty-seven-year-old photographer from Ohio who left her home town of Cincinnati when she was just seventeen, returned three years ago when she married someone who lives there, and is now taking care of her mom:

> One of the results of living here and being married here is that I'm the one who does the day-to-day stuff. She's basically okay, but things happen every week, and she has to go to the doctor, and I manage her life. And I feel like I'm meant to do it. Like it's okay. It's hard, and sometimes

it really is frustrating because she has a lot of short-term memory loss and she can't remember from one hour to the next what she said and she's pretty crazy, but basically she's okay.

In spite of the pressure and responsibility she feels in caring for her mom, Gwen, a Prodigal Daughter, views this as an opportunity to connect with her mom in a different way. Rather than feel anger and resentment toward her, especially given the history of their relationship, once distant and strained, Gwen is able to enjoy what her mom is capable of giving her at this point in their lives:

I really feel that there are very few things in my life where I knew I was supposed to be doing them, and this is one of them. So I feel that the other side of this is that I'm getting to know her in a slightly different way. She is grateful for my being here; she is more appreciative and a little mellower than she used to be in that she isn't ranting and raving all the time. She can do it pretty well still; however, she seems to appreciate me, which I never particularly felt in my life. So she's talking to me when we have lunch or when I'm at her place. She's telling me old stories; some of them I have never heard before.

Angela is prepared to relocate if necessary: "I concern myself with her health and if she is safe. I had my mother live with us when my daughters were in high school, but the altitude (10 thousand feet) and cold climate became difficult for her. I know at some point I may have to relocate to take care of her." Angela is the middle of three siblings and the oldest daughter.

No matter how much we sacrifice for our mothers or how dependent they are on us, some boomer daughters feel blessed to have their moms still in their lives. Carrie says, "I think she is terribly dependent on me, but I also know having her alive is very important to me at this stage in my life in undefinable ways—seeing my son grow up for one."

No matter how we as boomer daughters fought against the sacrifice our mothers made, we cannot help but be struck by the irony of life since we are now sacrificing for her.

The Sea of Guilt

One of the major frustrations for many of our respondents had to do with the stress of being their mother's mother. This is particularly true for working women with families. Our mothers sometimes do not fully appreciate all that we have to do. "She has made friends who will take her places but makes me feel that I've abandoned her when I suggest my busy schedule and job commitments," says Marjorie, a property manager and mother of one. "And of course, time for myself counts for nothing. She makes me feel guilty. Now I lie to her, and she survives when I do not make myself so available."

A thirty-seven-year-old waitress-actress-singer from Illinois says, "She's more dependent on me. At times I'm like her therapist, and at times it's draining." Another respondent, a forty-nine-year-old married mother of six and a full-time secretary from Canada, says of her mom, "We have switched roles. She cannot make a decision without my input. She uses the 'You're so much better at it' or 'I can't do that anymore' excuses. It's quite stressful."

Feelings of guilt run rampant with some boomer daughters, as with Mindy, mother of one and a dog sitter from Illinois: "I never had much to do with my mother as a teenager. As I can see it, her world is not as interesting as it was then. When she has feelings of isolation and boredom, I sometimes feel helpless. This scares me to death and makes me feel guilty if I do not help her." The guilt often intensifies when it comes to juggling mom's needs along with those of our own families. One respondent, a forty-seven-year-old teacher and the married mother of three from Illinois, says, "She's always been my strongest supporter. She hasn't been well lately, and I feel guilty that I don't see her more often. I know that she understands the obligations of a full-time job, a part-time job, a husband, and a young child." This respondent is the middle of three siblings and the oldest daughter.

Linda, the thirty-five-year-old magazine production manager from Vancouver, says, "I experience frustration at her seeming simplemindedness and her crabbiness when she is crossed. For the past three or four years, her deterioration has occupied our family quite a bit, but it is only in these recent years that I've felt irritation or condescension toward her, which makes me feel guilty sometimes."

Irritation is a dominant feeling many boomer daughters experience, especially in the early stages of their mothers' decline, as when our moms start telling the same family stories over and over again. Or we glance over and see her head nodding off in sleep, right in the middle of a birthday party or family get-together. Or because of impaired hearing, she continually interrupts our conversations with, "What? What'd you say?" Each time we have to repeat ourselves, our tone of voice becomes increasingly terse. And as each syllable rises in pitch, the waves of irritation swell and are followed by even larger waves of guilt. These wash over us with such intensity that we often feel as though we are drowning—drowning in sadness and despair. Our irritation is not really directed at her, but at the deterioration that is robbing us of the woman who has always been there for us, from the very first moment our life sparked in her body.

As we watch her deal with the ravages of nature as it wreaks havoc on her mind and body, we cannot help but wonder how Mother Nature will treat us in the latter stages of our lives. A thirty-six-year-old single account executive from Ohio says, "I worry about her a lot. She's not that well mentally or physically. She's very lonely. I worry about that because I know I'll be that way some day. She gave up most her friends when they got married. She's tired of going places on her own. It mirrors my life at an older age." Linda observes, "Recently my thoughts are of her failing memory and whether I carry the same traits." And Kate, who earlier spoke of her mom's unconditional love, says, "I worry most about her health and her fear of dying. She's had so many close calls with her heart. I've been with her at this time and it makes me think of my own mortality."

Saying Good-Bye

For most boomer daughters, the thought of our mothers' death, of of her absence, is too painful to hold for more than an instant. When it uninvited enters our consciousness, we meet it with fear, the intensity of which pushes it back to where it came from. As we shut it out, we might pick up the telephone, anxious to hear her voice, or maybe we search for her most recent letter or card in our junk drawer and gaze at her handwriting—something to confirm that she is still here.

Knowing how much she means to us and how she is nearing the end of her life's journey, we are filled with bittersweet emotions. As we reflect on her life—what she was and what she could have been, the hardships life doled out to her, what she sacrificed for us in the name of a mother's love (even with the most mediocre of motherly loves)—we feel a blend of deep gratitude and profound sadness. As our eyes burn with tears, we feel an empathy for this woman with graying hair and deeply furrowed skin, single breasted, fingers swollen with arthritis, or legs purpled by varicose veins. Our inherent gift of empathy, nurtured by her, periodically backfires when it comes to our moms, the only human being who knew us before we came into this world. It sometimes hurts too much to think about life without her. Sara, the thirty-nine-year-old administrative assistant from Illinois who earlier spoke of how difficult her mom's life was, says, "My mother and I have a wonderful relationship. I can talk to my mother about anything and never have to feel embarrassed. She is a wonderful woman. I don't know what I would do if anything happens to her, and when she dies, I know my life will suffer a void that no one or no thing can ever replace."

Colleen, a forty-eight-year-old divorced, unemployed mother of four from Colorado, says of her mom, "I have begun to realize that she will not be around forever, and I worry about her health and am afraid that she takes on too much and that her children and grandchildren expect and depend on her for too much. The worst fear I have is that I would not be able to deal with her death."

Other daughters feel they can let go: "Although my mother and I have some differences, I feel I have been a good daughter, attentive and caring. If my mother dies, I will shed tears of missing my best friend—not of guilt or regret. I know I did all I could to have a great mother-daughter relationship." Some are able to transcend the physical loss by holding on to the spirit of what their moms taught them. Julie, the thirty-six-year-old sales representative and a single mother of three from Illinois, says, "I am glad I have her to depend on. Everybody needs someone. Thank God that my mother is an even-tempered, unselfish woman. When I lived out of state, I thought about what I would do if my mother passed. I came to the conclusion that I would live and be the type of person she raised me to be: resourceful, insightful, caring, independent, and understanding. To stand tall! Be mannerly! Able! Respectful!"

Just as she helped us into the world, pushing hard, serving as our midwife in this thing called life, helping us to become caring, civilized human beings, we now help her as she goes out. We will be her midwife, helping her pull the threads of her life, of which we are but one, into a meaningful pattern.

Coming Home

*I try not to be so judgmental now and think about
how she must have been raised—with ten brothers
and sisters. They were children of immigrants, very
poor, and had very little education. But I love her.
She has some good points.*

> Marilyn, forty-two-year-old
> office manager and mother of two

I t has been a long, strange trip. We would not have believed this
could be so, especially when we were younger. But our relationship with our mothers—with its multiple wounds and still-healing
scars—can be mended. In the process, we are learning that we each
can revitalize the other.

Coming home to a peaceful spot in this bumpy journey has been
possible for the vast majority of our respondents and interviewees
because they could let go of the idealized mother. They have
decided it's time to embrace the real, live mothers they've got (and
who've got them), from whose bodies they sprang, and it's time to
let go of the unrealistic role models served up by our culture, like
the unruffled icons of 1950s television: Betty Anderson from *Father
Knows Best* and June Cleaver from *Leave It to Beaver*. It is possible
simply to love our mothers unconditionally. Although for some
respondents, this is a much greater challenge, given the neglect and

abuse they may have suffered at their moms' hands, they are able to differentiate the acts of mothering from the person providing them and appreciate their mothers as women within the context of their mothers' lives and the North American culture that shaped and limited them.

Acts of Courage

We can move our relationship with our moms to a deeper level or simply reach a comfortable, peaceful level in the space between us. But this requires an act of courage. The word *courage* is derived from the French word *cuer*, meaning "heart." The *Oxford English Dictionary* defines courage as "the heart as the seat of feeling, thought." We propose that we daughters muster the courage to forgive our mothers, to be compassionate toward them, and then to connect with them. After all, we share the same condition of being a female in a society where women have yet to achieve parity in pay scales or social status, where brave young women still bang on the doors of the elite Citadel military college, are allowed in only because of legal fiat, and then are sexually harassed for their troubles. We need to have a heart when it comes to our mothers.

That, we're pleased to report, is something the vast majority of our respondents possessed. They talked about the compassion they now feel for their mothers at this point in their relationships. Typical of this reconciliation is Doreen, who we met in Chapter Four. She believes that now, after all is said and done, "my mom did her best. I realize how difficult it must have been for her to raise me. Sometime in my thirties, my view of her shifted, so instead of seeing her as a terrible, cold bitch, I now see her as a half-formed person (just like I still am!) who never gave up on me despite what must have been terrible provocation."

Lily, a forty-five-year-old singer and songwriter from Illinois, reflects back on her tumultuous relationship with her now eighty-one-year-old mother, also a professional singer and as well a factory worker, babysitter, and caretaker of elderly people. When Lily was a teenager, she wasn't "allowed" to talk back, so she didn't. She remembers that her mother was moody and would sometimes stay in her bedroom with the shades down and the fan going, often crying. Lily didn't understand why. Nonetheless, Lily's mom encouraged Lily's unorthodox career path (while blaming Lily's father for preventing her from achieving her own career goals). Lily's mom also asked her daughter to leave home at seventeen and get on with her life and find a man. Lily did; she got married when she was only eighteen and then divorced. There's been a lot of water under the bridge for Lily and her mom. Still, this is what she sees at this point:

> My mom is strange and always has been, but she's basically a good person. She's made mistakes, but then so have I. We all have. She did the best she could with what she was given to work with. We're all limited physically, mentally, and emotionally. The one thing I have learned from all this is that we're all winging it. No one knows how their decision will turn out tomorrow, next week, let alone ten years down the road. You do what you think is best at the time and hope it's the right thing. It's not fair to condemn a parent for his or her mistakes. As an adult, you have the power to change your life. Your life is your responsibility.

The compassion shared by the majority of our respondents seems to be couched in unconditional love. Instead of thinking about whether we received unconditional love *from* her, we are able to take the trip back to her and begin to experience unconditional love *for* her. As we cease focusing on her shortcomings, gradually her strengths assume a more prominent role in our eyes. Jillian grew up in Northern Ireland, immigrating to Canada with her husband in her twenties, and has taught since 1965. Looking back on her relationship with her mother, she assesses it as distant when she was a child, neutral and sometimes oppositional as a teenager, and "reasonably close" in her midlife. Growing up, she felt that her mother rarely praised her, although her mom was always telling friends that her daughter was "so clever." After Jillian's marriage to a man her mother liked very much, both women worked harder on the relationship. "Perhaps my mother resented the fact that I often stuck up for my father when she was critical of him," Jillian recalls. "However, our relationship softened over the later years and was, perhaps, the best it had ever been. I wish I had made more attempts at being closer sooner. Perhaps I dwelled too much on the things she did that annoyed me and not so much on her good qualities, and there were many."

The Freedom in Forgiveness

Other daughters move to a greater degree of forgiveness by recognizing that our mothers are just one influence in our development as women. Cassie, a teacher and artist from Alberta, sums up her relationship with her mother as difficult—"my mother was extremely controlling and I allowed her to be"—but now assesses it this way: "My responses to the questions are unfair because they come at a time when Mother has become bitter and tired of the struggle and somewhat indifferent to me. All the buried resentments now leap into the light of day as though they are the only reality. They're not. Mother is a good, solid, honest, and sincere person who only wanted to do her best. I'm proud of who I am personally, but this didn't happen on its own. I am grateful for all the forces that have brought me to who I am."

The greatest difference between the Wandering Daughters and the Untraveled and Prodigals lies in this area of forgiveness. Prodigal and Untraveled Daughters no longer blame their moms for what they failed to give them. Marilyn and her mom had a rocky road to travel. Her mother was a Big Band singer in the forties, worked in an antiaircraft gun factory, and then "retired" to have her eight children. They fought all during Marilyn's adolescence. Marilyn blames her for being close-minded and sometimes cruel. But now, at forty-two, Marilyn is taking a step back:

> For many years I blamed her for so many bad things, like my low self-esteem. She used to make me feel small and ashamed with her belittling comments about my looks, my grades, my friends, my messy room, and so on. She used to call me stupid. I never shared my feelings with her because she didn't want to hear them, and she'd use it against me later. When I did something good, such as artwork, she was proud only because it made her look good to others. She wasn't very nurturing, once we started growing up and had a mind of our own. She didn't know how to deal with adolescents, so she yelled and hit us a lot. She never kept her promises and lied a lot. We didn't trust her to do what she said. But I try not to be so judgmental now and think about how she must have been raised—with ten brothers and sisters. They were children of immigrants, very poor, and had very little education. But I love her. She has some good points.

These daughters no longer focus on the "if onlys" and "what might have been." They no longer struggle over getting their mom's approval. For Wendy, a forty-one-year-old homemaker from Texas, all those fights as a teenager and her dream of being an artist, which her mother discouraged, are now seen in context:

> I love my mother; she will always will be my mother. But I have had to accept and deal with her disapproval of

me. I see my mother as very vulnerable, but I also now realize that she has always had difficulty expressing any emotion, except possibly anger. So much of what she told me and the way she treated me was an outgrowth of her own pain. And at least I understand that now. But her very conservative upbringing stifled so much of me that there is now very little I can see that was ever good advice. The only bright spot is that I believe I have been able to take the negatives I learned from her, see what SHOULD have been done for me, and apply that insight to my own life and parenting.

So after all those "if onlys" and approval seeking, these boomer daughters not only rest more comfortably in the space between their mothers and themselves but also in the space within. The waves of guilt, anger, and resentments have become mere ripples in the tides of emotions between their moms and themselves.

A Contextual View

Most of our respondents and interviewees were able to reach this level of forgiveness by seeing their moms within the context of their lives: the challenges their mothers faced, the sorrows they had to contend with, the limited horizons they may have faced. Jillian, in forgiving her mother, explains that her mom "had a hard life. Her mother died when she was four, and she was very poor. Then she had two children who left home and all but abandoned her. She was in a marriage with little love after the initial years."

It's simple but bears repeating: our mothers lived in different times. Many of our moms faced personal hardships and trials, the majority of them out of their control. Motherhood does not shield women from the adversities of life or give them any special advantage in being able to transcend the difficulties. Some of our respondents have come to believe that perhaps one of their mothers' greatest contributions to their daughters' lives revolves around how they learned to cope and muddle through. Now that the daughters have enough space and wisdom of their own, they may actually learn something from these trials from a different era. You could call this "historical perspective," as does Janis: "My mom has given me a historical perspective. She's lived long enough, been through and faced enough of life's challenges that just through her ability to cope with problems and losses head on, she's taught me the resiliency of the female spirit. I can now say to most things that come my way, 'Oh, I can get through this!'"

Still, our respondents cannot entirely put themselves back in their mothers' time and walk in their shoes. At the time our mothers were raising us, few respondents evaluated for us what was, in turn, influencing their mothers' mothering skills. Our mothers were limited to a narrower sphere of influence in the world, and their home (whether or not they had to go out and make some money) was the centripetal force in their lives, even though men still "ruled the roost" and, everyone knew, "a man's home was his castle." Given the limited options for women and the constriction of the female spirit, many of our moms lived in prisons of anger, resentments, and guilt that they frequently unleashed on their daughters. For, as we've seen that we share similarities with our mothers, guess who noticed it before we did? And so much of the negativity that mothers directed to us was really meant for themselves and, perhaps, the parts of themselves they saw in us—not just the genetic parts but the female parts that were devalued and sexualized by the wider culture, all of which contributed to their self-denigration. So, in addition to the hardships of life presented to our mothers—poverty, abuse, neglect, lack of education—they also had to contend with the adversity of being second-class citizens in a predominantly white male world, yet another source of anger.

The anger and rage we felt toward our mothers in the mid-1970s was expressed by Nancy Friday in her best-selling book of 1977,

My Mother/My Self. Friday spoke the words many of us felt at that point in our journey. Filled with criticisms, anger, hurt, and disappointment toward mothers in general as well as toward her own, Friday gives her own reconciliation with her mother the last three pages of her book, allowing that

> for every step I have taken away from her . . . I have been aware of her tugging at my heels, pulling me back. . . . It has taken me the entire writing of this book to acknowledge in my heart that the qualities I am proudest of in myself I learned from her. . . . In my absolutism about having made myself up out of no cloth taken from her, I have disinherited myself from my grandmother too. . . . In the service of maintaining a childish tie to a mother who never existed, I have turned my back on the best of my inheritance.

But Friday reverts back to the premise of her book by citing a male psychiatrist who questions the validity of her change of heart, charging that all this is mere "sentimentality, a defense against anger."

Baby boom women have changed so much around us, some by our mere numerical presence and some by design, that it's refreshing and no surprise that our respondents and interviewees appear to have decided (unbeknown to one another) to choose a new path in evaluating their relationships with their mothers. And they have decided to work toward sharing life with their mothers for as long as they are together or even beyond their mothers' deaths. This is a break with the traditional and patriarchal views of the mother-daughter connection. For if it's sentimentality that opens the door to our courage and allows us to be compassionate to our mothers as female human beings and to focus on our mothers' best selves, then we say, "Good!"

By coming home, bringing with us the lessons learned from the wider culture, we can joyfully embrace the feminine. We now realize that what we were looking for was closer at hand. Perhaps Joseph Campbell, mythologist and philosopher, says it best: "In the whole mythological tradition the woman is THERE. All she has to do is to realize that she's the place that people are trying to get to. When a woman realizes what her wonderful character is, she's not going to get messed up with the notion of being pseudo-male."

By forgiving our mothers, we are shifting to a new consciousness, one that has begun to embrace and truly value our feminine nature, yet is able to maintain a reasonable appreciation of the other side, the side that values the qualities of rationality, competition, independence, and achievement. This new consciousness is transforming us so that we can make choices for our lives that truly come from within our very nature, our center. The anger that drove us away from what our mothers and their lives represented is melting into a peacefulness that will allow us to make choices true to our own selves.

By forgiving our mothers, we become free to appreciate and support all women, regardless of their choices: whether it's to stay at home and raise children or to choose not to have children; whether it's to become a mother through a sperm donor or to be a corporate CEO. Many women feel a sense of shame and guilt in not working, or of having children and not being able to do it all, or of not having achieved greater success in their career paths, or of having a career but no children. This is often because that's what these women think other women are judging them on. It may be that all these women, busy assimilating into the wider culture and searching for the privileges associated with patriarchal values, have lost sight of their feminine side.

In the workplace, instead of competing with our female counterparts and holding tightly to the patriarchal values that encourage winning at all costs, we work with each other as partners and mutual supporters. Rather than continue to be motivated primarily by the search for the privileges associated with the dominant cultural values of competitiveness, independence, and emotional detachment, we can instead operate from within our own natural relational style, which favors the values of affiliation, nurturance, cooperation, and collaboration. Thus, we join with each other in being supportive and affirming.

The female relational style and the skills that support it are needed. In families, the feminine spirit nurtures and socializes its members, as our mothers did. In organizations, it helps individuals care not just about the bottom line but about the people who contribute to it. In the wider world, it helps people care about the environment and the creatures that inhabit it.

By acknowledging the feminine nature we share with other women, we truly come home.

Epilogue

We drove the secondary highways from Cincinnati to Hanover, Indiana, on a glorious May day to meet Carol Shields, who was the recipient of an honorary degree from her alma mater, Hanover College. Carol is one of North America's most celebrated writers: a Pulitzer Prize recipient, a finalist for the British Commonwealth's Booker Prize, a winner of Canada's Governor General Award. She is soft-spoken and unassuming, without the air of self-importance that weighs on so many other famous writers. Writing is simply one of the things she does, and now that her five children (one son and four daughters) are adults, she has even more time for this.

Shields is sixty, a half-generation older than the oldest of the baby boomer women, and has several grandchildren. She now looks at the divide between the generations and takes its measure:

> I can remember my mother sitting at the kitchen table and saying to the three of us (I have a brother and a sister): "You can be anything you want." In fact, even when she said that, I knew that I couldn't be anything that I wanted, and I am sure they did too, and she must have known too. I certainly was not in the period where girls rebelled against their families. We rebelled against nothing at all, but we went a bit further than our elders. We

had more education; we had more choices. Many women of that generation really didn't have any choices, and they didn't have much of a voice on who they were, and they didn't really, in a sense, claim their own lives. But I think that my mother knew very early that I was going to have quite a different life from hers—that I wasn't going to be like her, and yet, in a way I haven't had that different of a life. I married straight out of graduation. So I never had a job, and that was very traditional. And, in fact, no one said to me when I graduated, "Oh, what are you going to do next?" They knew what I was going to do: I was going to get married and have babies. Our lives were very predictable. On the other hand, my daughters have done exactly the same thing, yet they have gone further, and I think that maybe this is the way it works and that each generation goes a little further.

On the way back from our meeting with her, we talked quite a bit about what Carol said and wondered just how far the next generation, our daughters and daughters-in-law, might go. It was then that we decided that rather than speculate, we needed to seek out and talk with some young women who could give us the answers. We interviewed three young women, daughters of baby boomers, all charting a sure course for their careers and assuming that they can have families at the same time. We found they had high expectations of themselves—and of their mothers.

Melodie is a single twenty-one-year-old whose mom, a nurse, supervises a large, busy practice of ear, nose, and throat doctors. Her mom met her husband while in the Philippines during the Vietnam War, where she was stationed with the air force and rose to the rank of captain. As Melodie sees it, baby boomer women "were the pioneers of home and work and of bringing together home life and their careers. So for my generation, it's already pretty much assembled for us."

Many of us wouldn't disagree with Melodie. We *have* blazed the trail for bringing home and career together, which for most of us meant rejecting the stay-at-home mom our mothers represented. We decided to do it all and bring it together. Now, at midlife, we have arrived, and we have it all—career, family, and a burning hearth in our highly mortgaged houses—yet many of our respondents are asking the question: At what cost? As our daughters look at us, some of them pose the same question.

Ada is a successful, thirty-year-old marketing manager at a Fortune 500 company. She has an M.B.A.; her mother has a master's degree and is a university professor. In fact, looking at Ada's mother through Ada's description, one could evaluate the mother as highly accomplished but slightly intimidating. Ada's mom seems to have everything together. When Ada and her husband go back home for a visit, everyone is up at seven, busy working in the yard, going to the museum, running errands. Says Ada:

> My mom's incredible. She has a beautiful house, and the lawn is perfect, and she can cook fabulously. I mean she's incredibly talented, but at what cost? She never takes the time to realize that. I have to really work at being able to sit down, whether it's to watch TV or read, and just allow some time for myself to take care of myself. It's not easy. For my mom, there's always work to be done, and she's always complaining about it, and if I say, "Hey, Mom, you know that dust'll be there tomorrow. Why don't you just sit down and relax?" it angers her more than anything.

This feeling of always needing to do it all resonates with Melodie. She has a sophistication and understanding of relationships that would have been rare in her mother's generation. She nods as Ada recites the activities and accomplishments of her mother (and her father, a dean at a university), their children, their lives. Melodie wishes her mom would "chill":

I'd like to be able to sit in a room with my mom and talk about something without her mind and her body going in a million different directions at once. I wish she would slow down and stop and take a moment, because I don't ever see her do that. She knows that it really bothers me when I'm trying to talk to her and she's not listening. I'll stop talking and I'll say, "I hate when you do this!" and she'll realize what she's doing and say, "I know." But still, we haven't found a way to communicate where she can feel comfortable because I think she's uncomfortable in stillness, without that clatter or clutter.

It is not enough that her mother is listening; it is the quality of that listening that Melodie finds fault with: "A lot of times I don't feel like we're on the same wavelength. I feel that I'm pretty introspective anyway, and I feel like she doesn't have that quality in her. Like I honestly wonder if she ever thinks about things that are not on the surface. I don't know where she's integrating emotion and thought, and it's really frustrating."

Our third guest was Debra. An only child, her mother is also highly accomplished, having both a master's degree in health administration and an M.B.A. Like many other boomer women, she waited, until she was twenty-nine, to have Debra. Now a consultant, Debra's mother is divorced from her father; that difficult event is what Debra reckons has allowed their relationship—which was always close—to get even better:

These drastic changes really turned her inward, and she became more in tune with herself. She's got every how-to-be-good-to-yourself self-help book you could imagine. It really made her refocus her priorities because I think she was on this path, and I think I was on the same path, where it was like, succeed, succeed, succeed. We had to do well. That's how we proved ourselves. Three-piece suit with the little rosette. I think she really refocused her priorities, and she stopped and said, "Wait a minute. I don't like this." So it made *me* look and see I don't want to have to do that too.

Now, says Debra, not only has her mother "refocused," but, "I've learned so much from her. We can sit down and talk about this kind of stuff, about emotions. I think it took me seeing her at a vulnerable period in her life for us really to relate better. And now I trust her with anything. I've said some things to her about myself and my life that I can barely say to anybody else in the world."

From our surveys, we found that our respondents wanted more than anything to have better communication with their children, much more honest and open, much like Debra has with her mom. For Melodie and Ada, however, the depth of communication has been hampered by their moms' inability to take the time to just *be* with their daughters, fully focused on the time together. A more intimate level of one-on-one conversation devoid of distractions is clearly something these daughters wanted and expected.

They all commend their mothers for teaching them about social responsibility, honesty and integrity, compassion, concern for the environment, determination that they can do whatever they set their minds to, and generally for making it clear that their lives had great possibilities and their horizons were wide, particularly when it came to careers. Certainly they have a much wider choice than boomer women's own mothers could envision for us.

Nevertheless, it may be, as Debra, Ada, and Melodie point out, that the boomer generation needs to take some time out and to remember that even though we may have entered the world of work as a permanent feature of our lives, it may be limiting our ability to know ourselves apart from work and family. That requires that we think enough of ourselves to interrupt ourselves and stand back from the busyness in our lives. And it may be that this is something our daughters will do a better job at. As Melodie says of her mom,

"I do wish that she would slow down and savor the moment, because I don't ever see her doing that."

Much like our mothers' mantra was to get an education so we would have something to fall back on, we may need to tell our daughters to minister to themselves. Debra believes the greatest advice her mom has given her is just that: "To take care of yourself, take care of who you are. I think it's important because it acknowledges that you are a person, and as a self you are separate from the man you married, the children you have, and the job you have. You need to take care of your inner being."

There can't be any simple answers to the mother-daughter questions that each generation of daughters has asked. Mothers will never have a free ride; daughters will always wonder and ache about how mother could have done better. But if we look, we can see the spirit of our mothers within us, and in time we will cherish this connection, in spite of all the faults we attribute to her. And it will be a comfort, especially when she is no longer alive. Carol Shields, whose mother died in 1970, says:

> There is never a day when I don't think of my mother. I think of something she said, some little thing she did, the way she cooked something, the way she set the table. Something will come to me. And I just find it extraordinary that, in fact, what you do is you internalize your mother. I have a friend who just lost her mother this week, and it was a very close relationship, and she's trying to deal with it. I think this is what she'll find: that her mother will live on in *her* body, which is a curious thing when you think that we come from our mother's body. To me this is what's amazing.

Appendix A

Survey

If your mother died before you turned forty-five, please do not continue with this questionnaire.

We thank you for your interest in our project. We have kept the survey as short as possible so that it would not take too much of your time. Your responses will not only help us in gathering information, but they could possibly shed new light on your relationship with your mother.

I. DEMOGRAPHIC QUESTIONS
(Please fill in the blanks below)
(1) Age
(2) Marital Status
(3) Number of Children   Ages   Sex (M/F)

(4) Religion
(5) Race
(6) Highest Level of Education Attained
(7) State of Residence
(8) Current Profession/Occupation

(9) Work History (brief synopsis in two paragraphs or less)

(10) Age of Mother
     Age of Father
(11) Religion of Mother
     Religion of Father
(12) Highest Educational Level of Mother
     Highest Educational Level of Father
(13) Mother's Marital Status
     Mother's Marital History

     Father's Marital Status
     Father's Marital History

(14) Current Profession/Occupation of Mother

     Current Profession/Occupation of Father

(15) Mother's Work History (brief synopsis in two paragraphs
     or less)

     Father's Work History (brief synopsis in two paragraphs or less)

(16) In order of age, list your siblings by gender, including yourself.
Example:

Sibling	Age
Brother	58
Sister	50
Self	49

Sibling	Age
1. _____	_____
2. _____	_____
3. _____	_____
4. _____	_____
5. _____	_____

II. SURVEY QUESTIONS

This portion of the survey combines multiple choice and open-ended questions. For open-ended questions use additional paper if you need more space.

(17) When I was a teenager, my mother and I
   a. generally did not get along.
   b. got along all right.
   c. were neutral toward each other.
   d. other _____

(18) When I was a teenager, my mother and I
   a. fought openly about our disagreements.
   b. had silent wars with each other about our disagreements.
   c. communicated pretty openly and directly about our disagreements.
   d. rarely disagreed.
   e. other _____

(19) When I was a teenager, I thought my mother was
 a. pretty smart.
 b. of average intelligence.
 c. not very smart.
 d. I didn't think about it at all.
 e. other _____

(20) When I was a teenager, I thought my mother had
 a. high self-esteem.
 b. average self-esteem.
 c. low self-esteem.
 d. other _____

(21) When I was a teenager, I
 a. didn't want to be anything like my mother.
 b. didn't really care if I was anything like my mother.
 c. wanted to be just like my mother.
 d. other _____

(22) When I was a teenager, I thought my mother
 a. knew a lot about the world outside of her family.
 b. knew little of the world outside of her family.
 c. was primarily family focused.
 d. other _____

(23) When I was a teenager my mother positively (+) or negatively (−) or did not influence me (0) in the following areas:
 PLEASE CIRCLE

	Pos.	Neg.	Neutral
a. friendships with girls	+	−	0
b. relationships with boys	+	−	0
c. your self-confidence	+	−	0
d. your academic pursuits	+	−	0

e. your sexuality	+	–	0
f. your spiritual values	+	–	0
g. your body image	+	–	0
h. your capabilities	+	–	0
i. your ability to have fun and socialize	+	–	0
j. your dating life	+	–	0
k. your ability to be self-disciplined	+	–	0
l. other _____			

(24) At what age did you first realize you had similar traits to and/or qualities of your mother?

a. teens

b. twenties

c. thirties

d. forties

e. never

f. other _____

(25) Briefly describe the memory you have of this realization. What were you doing, who were you with, and how did you feel?

(26) At this point in my life, my mother and I

a. do not get along.

b. get along better than we did when I was a teenager.

c. are neutral toward each other.

d. have more problems than ever.

e. other _____

(27) At this point in my life, my mother and I
   a. fight openly about our disagreements.
   b. still have silent wars with each other about our
      disagreements.
   c. communicate pretty openly and directly about our
      disagreements.
   d. rarely disagree.
   e. other _____

(28) At this point in my life, I think my mother
   a. is pretty smart.
   b. has average intelligence.
   c. is not very smart.
   d. other _____

(29) At this point in my life, I see my mother as having
   a. high self-esteem.
   b. average self-esteem.
   c. low self-esteem.
   d. other _____

(30) At this point in my life, I
   a. still don't want to be anything like my mother.
   b. don't really care if I am anything like my mother.
   c. respect our differences but value many of my mother's
      qualities.
   d. want to be more like my mother.
   e. other _____

(31) At this point in my life, I see my mother
   a. interested in the world outside of her family.
   b. somewhat interested in the world outside of her family.
   c. primarily family focused.
   d. other _____

(32) At this point in my life, I see my mother as having positively
(+) or negatively (−) or not having any (0) influence on me
in each of the following areas:
PLEASE CIRCLE

	Pos.	Neg.	Neutral
a. my intimate relationships	+	−	0
b. my friendships	+	−	0
c. my feelings about career and work	+	−	0
d. my feelings about my parenting skills	+	−	0
e. my abilities to nurture self and others	+	−	0
f. my sexuality	+	−	0
g. my spirituality/spiritual values	+	−	0
h. my self-esteem	+	−	0
i. my self-confidence	+	−	0
j. my skills to manage finances	+	−	0
k. my ability to have fun	+	−	0

(33) At this point in my life, I
a. don't respect or value my mother.
b. neither respect nor disrespect my mother.
c. respect and value my mother.
d. other _____

(34) If your view of your mother has changed since you were a
teenager, describe what is different.

(35) At this point in time, my mother and I live in
    a. the same city.
    b. the same state but different towns.
    c. different states.
    d. different countries.

(36) At this point in my life, I
    (circle more than one if appropriate)
    a. talk to my mother every day by phone.
    b. would talk to my mother every day if we didn't live so far apart.
    c. talk to her once or twice a week by phone.
    d. write to her frequently.
    e. write to her infrequently.

(37) When we communicate (circle more than one if appropriate),
    a. I mostly initiate the phone calls.
    b. my mother mostly initiates the phone calls.
    c. we equally initiate phone contact.
    d. my mother writes more frequently.
    e. other _____

(38) I see my mother
    a. 4–7 times a week.
    b. 1–3 times a week.
    c. a few times a month.
    d. once or twice a year.
    e. other _____

(39) Regardless of the quality of your relationship with your mother, how often do you find yourself thinking about her or your relationship with her?
    a. daily
    b. weekly
    c. monthly
    d. never

(40) Briefly summarize just what your most frequent thoughts about her are.

(41) Do you see yourself as being too dependent in your relationship with her?
   a. yes
   b. no
   c. sometimes

(42) If you answered yes or sometimes, briefly describe how you feel about this dependency.

(43) List the clichés, favorite sayings, homilies, or quips your mother did or still does frequently communicate to you. (For example: "Nice girls don't swear or smoke." "It's not what you say; it's how you say it.")

(44) Describe how you have been most influenced by your mother in one of the following categories: *Sense of Self; Education; Career; Relationships with Men/Women; Parenting; Self-Confidence; Friendship; Finances; Creativity; Spirituality; Sexuality; and Leisure/Recreation.*

(45) What is the greatest piece of advice your mother ever gave you?

(46) Why do you consider it to be so great?

(47) What's the worst piece of advice your mother ever gave you?

(48) Why do you consider it the worst?

(49) At this point in your life, as you reflect on your relationship with your mother, is there anything you think she was right about that you once may have discounted? Please include your feelings about reflecting on this question.

(50) How much do you know about your mother's background and history (before she became a mother)?

(51) Is there a particular value or characteristic that your mother passed along to you, either through her words or her actions, that you have or would like to have passed along to your daughter(s)? (If you don't have any daughters, what would you have liked to pass along?)

(52) If you have any additional comments regarding your
relationship with your mother that you would like to share,
please do so below.

Appendix B

What Our Mothers Told Us:
A Cliché for Every Occasion

Mom on Dating, Men, Sex, and Marriage

Why buy the cow when he can get the milk for free?

It's a man's world.

Men are like buses. If you miss one, you can always catch another one.

Trust no man completely.

Absence makes the heart grow fonder.

The most important thing in life is love.

Once bitten, twice shy.

Boys only want one thing.

For every old sock, there's an old shoe.

Nice girls play hard to get.

Listen to your heart.

Don't wear your heart on your sleeve.

You don't have to love a man to go out with him.

It's just as easy to marry a rich man as a poor one.

A bad reputation is the hardest thing to live down.

Nice girls don't do that.

The best birth control pill is an aspirin between your knees.

Don't do anything with a boy you wouldn't do in front of your parents.

Stay together for the children.

Mom on Appearance

Pretty is as pretty does.

Wear something in good taste, not high fashion.

Always wear decent clothes when you go out of the house.

Women over forty shouldn't wear hair styles below their shoulders.

You're not really dressed unless you're wearing makeup.

Don't wear patent leather and white shoes before May 31 or after Labor Day.

Beauty is in the eye of the beholder.

Always wear clean underwear.

Do the best you can to make yourself look good; then don't think about it.

Beauty comes from within.

It's not your fault if you're not beautiful at fifteen, but it is when you are fifty.

If you've got it, flaunt it.

Good posture will take you everywhere.

A lady never lets her shoes wear out.

Get that hair out of your eyes. Your face is too pretty to hide.

Don't make that face; it will stick.

You can't make a silk purse out of a sow's ear.

Mom on Social Etiquette, Social Skills, or "Do the Right Thing"

Don't talk with your mouth full.

Good breeding consists of how much we think of ourselves and how little we think of the other person.

It's neither the time nor the place.

If everyone else jumped off a bridge, would you follow?

If you can't say anything nice, don't say it at all.

Treat others the way that you would like to be treated.

Don't stare; it's not polite!

Manners don't cost money; therefore you must have good ones.

What comes around goes around.

Oh what a tangled web we weave when first we practice to deceive.

Nobody likes a showoff.

Shut your mouth, and open your ears.

What will the neighbors think?

Sticks and stones will break my bones, but names will never hurt me.

Nosy people don't live long.

You can't change the world.

The mills of the grind go slowly but they grind exceedingly fine.

Mom on Spirituality and Religion

I'll pray for that.

Keep the faith.

Put it in God's hands. He'll fix it.

We can live abundantly through Christ.

Things happen for a reason.

Count your blessings.

Prayer is powerful.

Whenever God closes a door, he opens a window.

Say the rosary.

The church says . . .

Offer it up.

In God, all things are possible.

Mom on Finances and Penny-Pinching

Waste not, want not.

Don't talk about money.

They have old money and they have new money, but it all spends the same.

It's not how much you earn, it's how you handle it that counts.

The more you earn, the more you spend.

If it can be fixed with money, it's not a serious problem.

Caveat emptor.

Rich beyond the wildest dreams of avarice.

Neither a borrower nor a lender be.

A penny saved is a penny earned.

Save the pennies, and the pounds will take care of themselves.

Willful waste brings woeful want.

Poor people have poor ways; them's that have, gets.

You get what you pay for.

Mom's Threats and Curses

You made your bed; now lie in it.

Pride goeth before the fall.

Do as I say, not as I do.

Because I said so.

Don't talk to strangers.

I don't care what so and so does, I'm not her mother, I'm yours, and I care about you.

It's going to hurt me more than it does you.

Who do you think you are?

You don't have to love me, but you will respect me.

Children should be seen and not heard.

Don't tell your father.

I didn't raise you that way.

When children are small, they step on your feet; when they are big, they step on your heart.

As long as you live under this roof, you'll do as I say.

Wait 'til your father gets home.

Respect your elders.

That's the rock you'll perish on.

You'll rue the day.

Wait until you have children!

Mom on Education

Go to college.

Learn a second language.

Good grades are their own reward.

It's better to have it and not need it than to need it and not have it.

Get a good education so you have more than I did.

If you don't study, you'll end up a washerwoman.

Get your education; once you have it, no man can take it away.

Don't let anyone know you are intelligent—that's arrogant.

Don't be a dummy like me. Go to college.

Mom as the Martyr

There are givers and takers (I'm a giver).

The stress you girls give me caused my diabetes [or whatever other condition she may have].

If I could only get my head above water.

You have everything; I have nothing.

I have tried to do all I could do.

Mom on Health and Fitness

Moderation in all things.

Don't overdo.

Get some rest.

Do something for yourself.

Eat lots of salads and vegetables.

Eat less red meat.

Use lots of garlic.

You are what you eat.

You must drink eight glasses of water each day.

When you're through improving yourself, you're through.

Save your feet.

Don't trust doctors.

Eating carrots will make your eyes sparkle.

No sun.

Too much sun causes cancer.

Eating bread crusts will give you curly hair.

When are you going to lose weight?

Mom on Independence

Always be your own person.

It's great standing on your own two feet.

Mom on People

A leopard doesn't change its spots.

People love to talk about themselves: listen and learn.

Always give people the benefit of the doubt.

"Everyone to his own taste," the old woman said as she kissed the cow.

Don't criticize others until you are perfect yourself.

A rolling stone gathers no moss.

The rich get richer; the poor get children.

Mom on Housekeeping and Cleanliness

A job worth doing is worth doing right the first time.

A little bit of dirt never hurt anyone.

When I come to your house, you can do it that way.

Dull women have to clean houses.

Don't put wet things on dry things.

Tidy as you go along.

Mom on Work, Career, and Productivity

Don't quit your job until you have another one lined up.

Do something you love to do; then you'll meet others who have the same interests.

A job worth doing is a job worth doing well.

Always do the best job to the best of your ability.

Always put in a full day's work.

A stitch in time saves nine.

The early bird gets the worm.

You can do anything you want if you try.

I knew you could do it.

He who hesitates is lost.

Slow and steady wins the race.

All I can say is, "Do your best."

Be the best you can be.

You're not living up to your potential.

Time's a wastin'.

Mom on Family

You can't be mad. It's family.

Don't have babies for me.

You should call your father.

A chip off the old block.

A nut doesn't fall far from the tree.

Don't tell our family business to anyone.

A son's a son 'til he takes a wife, but a daughter's a daughter for the rest of your life.

Blood is thicker than water.

Why can't all of you [siblings] get along?

You're your father's daughter.

Friends come and go, but your family's there no matter what.

Babies are not romantic.

What goes on in this house stays in this house.

Mom on Dealing with Life

Look at the bright side.

Every cloud has a silver lining.

Time will tell.

You have to take the bitter with the sweet.

You make your own happiness.

All good things take time.

Listen to your heart and not your head.

Don't sweat the small stuff.

To your own self be true.

Life is what you make it.

Disappointments build character.

Don't count your chickens before they hatch.

You don't miss what you never had.

Don't be so hard on yourself.

It could have been worse.

The road to ruin is often paved with good intentions.

Live one day at a time.

First things first.

Never say never.

Enjoy your life; it is the only one you have.

No news is good news.

Whoever told you life was fair?

You never miss the water 'til the well runs dry, and you'll never miss your mother 'til she's gone.

Make a good first impression.

Out of sight, out of mind.

Listen to your mother; she's always right.

Mom on Humor

Oh shoot! That's a pistol.

Funny ha, ha or funny weird?

Just in the nicotine [nick-of-time]!

Mom on Friendship

Birds of a feather flock together.

Stay out of people's houses. Why do you think I pay rent here?

You have to pick better friends.

Why are you hanging around those folks?

Lie down with dogs, get up with fleas.

Notes

Chapter One

P. 4, *Nancy Friday's best-selling book:* Friday, N. (1977). *My mother/ my self.* New York: Dell.

P. 6, *One central feature is that women:* Baker Miller, J. (1986). *Toward a new psychology of women* (2nd ed.). Boston: Beacon Press.

P. 6, *Relationships, and particularly issues of dependency:* Gilligan, C. (1982). *In a different voice: Psychological theory and women's development.* Cambridge, MA: Harvard University Press.

Chapter Two

P. 28, Life *magazine featured a bizarre photo: Life.* (1946, January 7). p. 10.

P. 28, *the first winter of peace:* Grim Europe faces winter of misery (1946, January 7). *Life,* p. 45.

P. 28, *In the 1940s, condoms and douching:* Factors affecting fertility. (1962). In C. Kiser (Ed.), *Research and family planning.* Princeton, NJ: Princeton University Press; United States method of fertility control, 1955, 1960, 1965. (1967, February). *Studies in Family Planning,* no. 17.

P. 29, *Bernard Asbell, in his history:* Asbell, B. (1995). *The pill.* New York: Random House.

P. 29, *In a 1947 article in the* American Journal of Obstetrics: Cited in Asbell, B. (1995). *op cit.*

P. 29, *In a 1946 ad for Modess: Life.* (1946, February 21). p. 91.

P. 30, *Eleanor Roosevelt in the pages of* Ladies': Roosevelt, E. (1946, January). If you ask me. *Ladies' Home Journal*, p. 20.

P. 30, *It may seem unbelievable now:* More doctors smoke Camels than any other cigarette. (1947, March). *Ladies' Home Journal*, p. 21.

P. 30, But, *mom had to beware dishpan hands:* How John hated his boss to see my dishpan hands [advertisement]. (1947, February). *Ladies' Home Journal*, p. 22.

P. 31, *Says Basinger, "The woman's film:* Basinger, J. (1993). A woman's view: How Hollywood spoke to women, 1930–1960. New York: Knopf.

P. 32, *In fact, Bureau of the Census figures show:* U.S. Bureau of Labor Statistics. (1972). *Marital status of women in the civilian labor force: 1890 to 1970.* Washington, DC: Government Printing Office.

P. 32, *In an address to the graduates of Smith College:* Stevenson, A. (1974). *The papers of Adlai E. Stevenson* (Vol. 4). (W. Johnson, Ed.). Boston: Little, Brown.

P. 33, *In a 1948 survey of its members:* vom Baur Hansl, E. (1948). Questionnaire to AAUW graduates. *American Association of University Women, 44*(3), 499–500.

P.34, *Following three carefree roommates:* Three carefree girls from Missouri. (1946, January). *Ladies' Home Journal*, p. 47.

P. 34, *Film critic Molly Haskell argues that Hollywood:* Haskell, M. (1974). *From reverence to rape: The treatment of women in the movies.* Chicago: University of Chicago Press.

P. 34, *Or, as Jeanine Basinger puts it:* Basinger, J. (1993). *ibid.*

P. 35, *Even if everything had gone according:* Roosevelt, E. (1947, June). If you ask me. *Ladies' Home Journal*, p. 28.

P. 37, *Landon Y. Jones argues:* Jones, L. (1980). *Great expectations: America and the baby boom generation.* New York: Ballantine.

P. 37, Time *magazine, in a cover story called:* To heal a nation. (1969, January 24). *Time*, p. 22.

P. 38, *the American film's view of woman:* Haskell, M. (1979). *ibid.*

P. 39, *In 1968, a University of California coed and a member of the Communist Party:* Education. (1965, December 3). *Time*, p. 17.

P. 41, *As Bernard Asbell says in* The Pill: Asbell, B. (1995). *ibid.*

P. 41, Ladies' Home Journal *celebrated the Pill's:* Cunningham, A. (1990, June). The pill: How it changed our lives. *Ladies' Home Journal,* p. 121.

Chapter Five

P. 87, *highlighted by the fact that time spent on homemaking:* Dubeck, P., & Borman, K. (Eds.). (1996). *Women and work: A handbook.* New York: Garland.

P. 101, *Recent studies estimate that representative values:* Dubeck, P., & Borman, K. (Eds.). (1996). *op cit.*

Chapter Six

P.110, *In 1955, according to the Princeton Religion Research Center:* Bezilla, R. (Ed.). (1996). *Religion in America, '96.* Princeton, NJ: Princeton Religion Research Center.

P. 111, *According to the National Council of Churches:* Jacquet, Jr., C. (1988, September). *Women ministers in 1986 and 1977: A ten year view.* New York: National Council of Churches of Christ in the USA.

P. 111, *The Hartford Study of 1996 noted:* Zikmund, B. B., Lummis, A., & Chang. (1997). *An uphill calling: Clergy women and men in the contemporary Protestant church.* Westminster, CT: John Knox Press.

P. 111, *Nonetheless, a survey of female leadership in religion:* Niebuhr, G. (1996, December). Religion. *Working Woman,* p. 25.

P. 120, *As Shaun McNiff argues in his wonderful book:* McNiff, S. (1995). *Earth angels: Engaging the sacred in everyday things.* Boston: Shambhala.

P. 123, *In a 1946 issue of:* Tasty food. (1946, March). *Ladies' Home Journal;* Kelley, J. (1996). A French country Christmas. *Bon Appetit,* p. 71.

Chapter Eight

P. 159, *Looking at what mother may or may not have:* Friday, N. (1977). *My mother/my self.* New York: Dell.

Chapter Nine

P. 173, *that set out to discover:* Gilligan, C. (1982). *In a different voice: Psychological theory and women's development.* Cambridge, MA: Harvard University Press.

P. 174, *Relationships between parents and children are:* Baker Miller, J. (1986). *Toward a new psychology of women.* Boston: Beacon Press.

Chapter Eleven

P. 212, *for every step I have taken away from:* Friday, N. (1977). *My mother/my self* (p. 458). New York: Dell.

P. 212, *sentimentality, a defense against anger.* Friday, N. (1977). *op cit.*, p. 455.

P. 213, *Joseph Campbell:* Moyers, B. (1988). *Joseph Campbell: The power of myth* (Audiotape). Produced by High Bridge in association with *Parabola, The Magazine of Myth and Tradition.*

Index

About the Authors

Barbara McFarland is a psychologist and has been in private practice for twenty years working primarily with adolescent and adult women with a focus on eating disorders. She has authored numerous books and articles, including *Shame and Body Image, Feeding the Empty Heart,* and *Brief Therapy and Eating Disorders.* She conducts workshops for both professionals and laypersons. The mother of one son, she lives with her spouse, Harold, and their dog, Fred, on their farm in Burlington, Kentucky.

Virginia Watson-Rouslin is a freelance writer in Cincinnati, Ohio, who has written about subjects ranging from women sports reporters in the locker room to divorce lawyers. She has been a book and magazine editor, a television producer, and, for nine years, a public affairs officer for the Canadian Consulate at the trade office in Cincinnati, where, among other duties, she helped promote Canadian writers and artists in the Midwest. She is currently a communications and marketing consultant. She lives with her husband, William Rouslin, and Petroushka, their awesome Siberian husky, in Montgomery, Ohio.